SAMANTHA CLARKE is a happiness consultant, founder of the Love It or Leave It movement, and lecturer at The School of Life where she facilitates workshops on career potential, building a portfolio career, managing stress and confidence.

Samantha works directly with company HR, leaders and managers to develop happiness strategies and coaching initiatives that spark better conversations around personal career growth and wellbeing at work, and has worked with a range of successful brands such as Innocent, MediaCom UK, Deutsche Telekom, Dishoom, Viacom, The Royal Bank of Scotland, Pepsico, American Express, British Fashion Council and more.

She regularly gives keynote speeches and has delivered talks for Design Hotels AG, Harrods, Giorgio Armani, University of Cambridge, Cannes Lions, *Stylist* Live, *Elle* Weekender, the Abu Dhabi Government HR summit and the Soho House Group.

Samantha has a podcast series called 'Love It or Leave It', which features interviews with philosophers, start-up founders, workplace food designers, tech experts and more. Her work has been covered by *Monocle*, *Stylist*, *The Times*, *Psychologies*, *Forbes*, *Harper's Bazaar*, *Elle*, *Evening Standard*, *City AM*, BBC Global News and BBC Radio 4.

To discover more, visit www.loveitleaveit.co.

@samanthaand_ and @_loveitleaveit_

Praise for Samantha's work:

'I loved the Love It or Leave It session with Samantha. It was full of lots of useful and practical tips. I'd definitely recommend Samantha to others.'

Naomi Puri, Talent Acquisition Manager, Royal Bank of Scotland

'As a coach, Samantha brings a thoughtful, well-researched approach to her practice. Her calm, grounding and easy-going style helps you feel safe to step outside your comfort zone and perform at your best. Readers can expect actionable advice that stirs their thinking, challenges their assumptions and ultimately helps them do more work that matters (and less of the work that doesn't).'

Perri Lewis, co-founder and CEO, Mastered

'Samantha is a very knowledgeable and experienced expert on work happiness.'

Serdar Kutucu, Chief Operating Officer, Design Hotels AG

'We couldn't have picked a better person to raise the happiness levels of our employees.'

Josh Krichefski, EMEA CEO, MediaCom UK

'Samantha helped our general managers and head chefs better understand what it is that makes them happy and how they can achieve more happiness in their lives and with their teams. It certainly was a worthwhile investment. Samantha is awesome!'

Andy O'Callaghan, Head of People, Dishoom

LOVE IT OR LEAVE IT

HOW TO BE HAPPY AT WORK

SAMANTHA CLARKE

ENDEAVOUR

To everyone who is on a path searching for fulfilling, purposeful, meaningful, healthier and happier ways to work and be, this book is for you…

An Hachette UK Company
www.hachette.co.uk

First published in Great Britain in 2020 by Endeavour, an imprint of
Octopus Publishing Group Ltd
Carmelite House
50 Victoria Embankment
London EC4Y 0DZ
www.octopusbooks.co.uk

ISBN 978 1 91306 808 0

A CIP catalogue record for this book is available from the British Library.

Printed and bound in the UK

10 9 8 7 6 5 4 3 2 1

CONTENTS

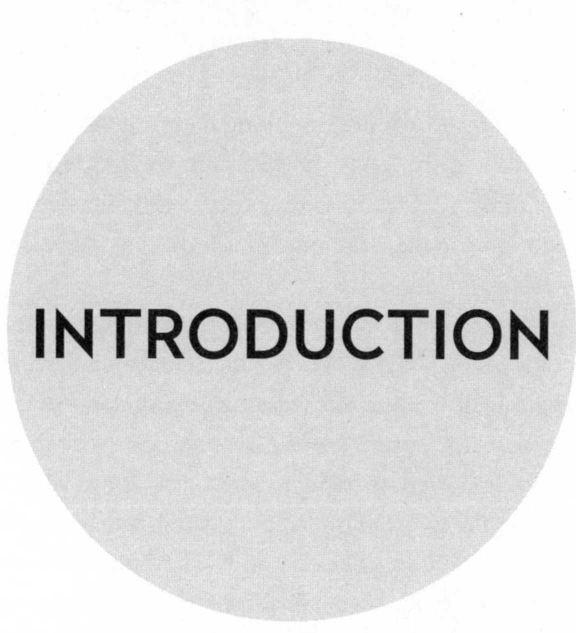

INTRODUCTION

Work: what's happened to you? You've changed.

Our relationship with work is a bitter, twisted love story. We started out exchanging muscle time in the fields for dollars. Work was brutal, hard and joyless. Then we came in from the cold and into the warmth of the office. Here our relationship with work flourished as we acquired smarts and technical skills. We were inquisitive; hungry to see where the relationship would take us. So much so that we let the relationship engulf us: trading our time and brains for money, we gave even more of our time to work in the hope of a brighter future.

Slowly but surely our work started to get a bit clingy, hanging off our every interaction, stalking us in our downtime and toying with our emotions. Hopeless and confused, we gave in, allowing it to get in the way of our sleep, our sex lives and squashing our personalities at parties. We find ourselves now in a tricky situation with work as it's not so easy to ghost it. Even when we try to move on and do things in a new way, it keeps reminding us of how far we've come together, what we would be throwing away, all the trappings we bought and can buy with it, and how our identities and happiness are inextricably linked (I delve into this a lot deeper in Chapter 1).

On top of this, other forces are pounding on our relationship with work, urging that we wake up from our slumber and demand more from this relationship. Technology is transforming our work life faster than we can keep pace. Each of us in this relationship is having to shapeshift and make some new decisions.

As with any relationship, you can't just look at it through one lens only, and there is also a positive side to this changeable dynamic. While technology might be throttling our working potential in one direction, it's softened up parameters around *how we work* and pushed our creativity in generous ways. It's given us freedom and flexibility to work remotely, edit documents on the go from our phones, bring our wildest imaginable ideas and curiosities to life and build bonds with individuals in multiple time zones. While these qualities will allow you to expand your work opportunities, as we will see later on in Chapter 10, for now I want to focus on what the darker side of technology is doing to shape your working life.

Work will be OK. It's got many options ahead of it. It's most likely that in the not-too-distant future many industries will increasingly use AI, so it will be YOU who needs to define your status in this relationship before it is too late.

There are areas technology cannot compete in (at present), such as our natural human abilities. For example, your creative and innovative vision, empathy, and critical and strategic thinking. Technology will take no prisoners in some job roles. You can see this currently when you walk into a bank or a supermarket which used to be teeming with staff who have now been replaced by machines. In this instance the machines may be quicker, but the human element has been streamlined. Maybe your job hasn't been automated as quickly as this, but that doesn't mean you should sit back. Whether you are working with technology or developing it, or in a very human-specific role, now is the time for you to get smarter, sharper and progressive with how you think about your skills for future roles.

Have you figured out who you will become after the break-up?

Sounds a bit drastic, but work has changed and will continue to morph – so it's time that you did your due diligence to take the best steps forward. Owning who you are and identifying your signature superhero qualities will help you stay ahead of the curve.

Can you be a change acrobat?

From a neurological point of view, the older we get the more our brains are resistant to change. Change isn't comfortable, it's messy and our brains don't like it. But change and adapt you must. Doing an audit of where you are, where you want to get to and what you need to take you there will be pivotal to your future.

You may think I'm just talking about skills here but I'm not. Becoming more technically astute is old hat; you can't outpace AI. Rather than pushing into the headwind, it's easier to follow the path of least resistance and power up in another way. A good start is to develop those often-mocked personal soft skills. The future will demand that you know how to:

- Dance through challenges with ease
- Empathize and be of service to others
- Problem-solve like a beast
- Collaborate and build relationships with new and old contacts
- Manage your own emotional and mental wellbeing for success
- Communicate effectively both in person and across digital platforms
- Be socially influential and lead not only others but yourself

There seems to be a new term every day to represent just how much work is shifting: gig working, portfolio careers, remote working. Not to forget liquid talent. The term 'liquid talent' has been coined by companies keen to create a pool of talent that they can dip in and out of in flexible ways to get help with ad hoc projects. The future workforce will be a motley crew of contractors, freelancers, AI, robots and pools of liquid, outsourced talent.

Are you able to develop new habits that will make you bendy, stretchy and open to whatever blows your way?

This book will be your cod liver oil prescription to help you limber up and get flexy! Getting a head start in the race means being continuously open to learning, spotting opportunities on the horizon and preparing yourself mentally and physically.

What led you to this book?

Curiosity? A whim? A recommendation from a loved one? Are you tired of insubstantial career resources? For whatever reason, this provocative title has found its way into your hands and I've created a book with a flow that will help you make real moves whether you want to Love It or Leave It.

> 'Love It' – find ways to fall in love with your current role and cultivate your work happiness inside your existing job as well as outside of it.
>
> Or
>
> 'Leave It' – harness a better work identity, parcel up your skills and move on to something else. Whether that's retraining, a new job, a portfolio career or testing a business.

I want you to read through both paths and think consciously about how you feel about each. There is no right or wrong when it comes to the path you choose but at least you'll be clued up to make the appropriate choice. I'm an impartial advisor, here to ask provocative questions about your future work happiness, to help clear the weeds from the paths but not to push you towards one side or the other. The choice is ultimately yours.

My recommendation is that you read through all the steps in one go and make notes as you go along rather than skipping to chapters that tickle your fancy (which can seem like the easier, tempting option, but it's not the best). There are exercises throughout the book to help you get thinking about your options.

By using the roadmap I've created in this book you will get more clarity on how to redesign your relationship with work and yourself. I want you to show 'work' that you mean business. To find your happiness, you need to be as prepared as possible and know that there are no quick fixes. Be open to shining a light on the dusty corners of your work relationship to find the change you've been seeking.

Time is of the essence!

SECTION 1:
WORK / LIFE HARMONY

CHAPTER 1

WHO THE HELL AM I?

You're at a party or dinner and someone turns around and asks, 'So what do you do?'

What's your initial reaction? Do you shy away from it? Nervously navigate the dance of whose job is better? Or perhaps hide that you're jealous of someone working remotely in a field you wish you were in? Or do you get defensive or negative about the humdrum of work? CEO, designer, lawyer, doctor... titles like these have kept some of us hemmed in and stifled for too long and yet it is what we continuously use to judge each other.

I want you to repeat after me: I AM NOT MY TITLE. I AM NOT MY TITLE. I AM NOT MY TITLE.

Who are you?

From a company perspective, the label you are given serves to help them:

- Organize you and sort you like cattle
- Set clear markers to everyone else of what your remit of expertise and seniority is
- Make the recruitment officer's life easy
- Clarify your pay bracket

But it hems you in by:

- ➤ Putting blinkers on your ambition
- ➤ Restricting your ability and dumbing down your skills and capabilities
- ➤ Fuelling office drama when someone tries to operate above their station

When all is said and done, your title is yesterday's news. Yes, you heard me. Nobody cares. Job titles are a revolving door. Virtual Reality Curator, Urban Farmer, Memory Surgeon... heard of these before? No? Well, they are coming soon, so resist the temptation to pin your hopes and identity to a title or its current glossy meaning because poof! It will be gone tomorrow.

Move over pigeonholed job roles or descriptions and say hello to a web of adaptable skills, capabilities and competencies. It will be up to you to weave together a mix of skills or to collect mini job experiences that will show future employers who you are. I call this mix of skills and experiences the 'work umbrella'.

I'll explain more on how to do this later, but here's a little thought starter: what might be an alternative 'work umbrella' that describes what you could do, if you had free rein? I'll take myself as an example:

Happiness consultant – helping individuals and companies make work happiness a priority.

My umbrella term runs the gamut of writing, podcasting, public speaking, coaching, consulting, leading a team, financial management, strategizing, problem-solving, curating and creating. Need I say more?

So rather than just sticking with 'UX designer' or 'doctor' or 'writer', what else might you be and how do you want to describe it? Don't worry if you feel as if I've just thrown you into the deep end, we will cover it in more detail later on. I've got you!

When all you've got is work (in your life)

There is a wider issue beyond the fact that we've put so much stock into job titles that feel like a cashmere jumper we've let slip into the standard wash (shrunken, ill-fitting and small). Work has sucked all of the life out of us, so much so that we've forgotten how to have fun, to play, to experiment.

What else is going on in your life apart from work?

When all we have is work, what happens if suddenly it all goes up in smoke? I've coached individuals in the past who've been made redundant or were sacked suddenly and they often have a sharp realization of just how narrow and tailored their world had become. Their ecosystem was tied solely to work, it's where most of their friends were as well as their self-esteem and purpose. When we tie our work and our identity into a neat little bundle like this, we end up allowing all of our challenges and frustrations with co-workers or the job role to consume our minds and take everything so damn personally. Our preoccupation with work keeps us far from present with our friends, family and the other beautiful things life has to offer.

In some cases, we begin to base our entire existence on meeting and finding people, events and relationships that are purely for the advancement of our careers. This is a crazy way to live! When you continue to withdraw from your life in favour of investing more into those work hours, you end up like a broken Easter egg left on the shelf after Easter.

Let's have a go at correcting this. In terms of being present, just understanding yourself and your actions is one piece of a larger jigsaw of work happiness. There is also the relationships you have with other people in your life and what I would consider most important – your home.

How is work slapping the life out of you?

The reality of sitting alone with our thoughts is often the last thing we'd choose to do, but it's what's necessary to make sure we own who we are and our work happiness. Individuals today are terrified of the spaces or silences in which questions about who they are might surface and they do their best to drown them in distractions. Pick your poison: whether it is scrolling through social media feeds, distraction shopping or another beer in the pub, we do anything to avoid staring our work problems in the face.

EXERCISE

The sweet spot

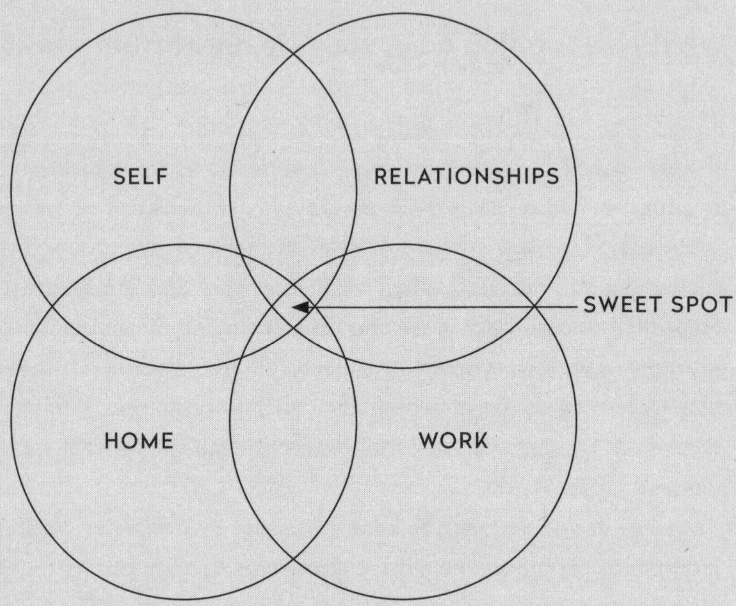

By assessing the four zones – Self, Relationships, Home and Work – you can recalibrate and make changes that are meaningful to your wellbeing.

Grab a pen and get comfy. I want you to actively work through and answer the questions. Writing your answers down will help you see in black and white what's really going on, and usually helps generate those light-bulb moments.

If you are scared, I get that! But I'm urging you to hold a mirror up to yourself today and answer these questions truthfully. It will serve you better in the long run if you can see the full picture of where you are right now, so that you can understand clearly where you need to go.

Self

When was the last time you allowed yourself to just play?

I love the idea that play helps us to get inquisitive, chill the hell out, create and just laugh. But we've become so serious and wedded to our job that it has stamped out the fun. Pssst… your friends and family are just too shy to tell you, but it's true, you've become a boring workaholic.

> *'Life without play is a grinding, mechanical existence organized around doing the things necessary for survival. Play is the stick that stirs the drink. It is the basis of all art, games, books, sports, movies, fashion, fun, and wonder – in short, the basis of what we think of as civilization. Play is the vital essence of life. It is what makes life lively.'*
>
> **Stuart Brown (renowned psychiatrist from the Institute of Play)**

How does your body and spirit feel?
Suffering from any migraines, neck and shoulder pain? Any pain you're experiencing is your body's way of telling you it needs a break and some attention. Most of the time we push through and carry on. STOP! If your spirit is low or tiredness seems to be your Groundhog Day reality, it's time to realize that your brain is overloaded and heading to meltdown zone.

When it comes to your work/life choices, which priorities are yours and which are other people's?
You are such a people pleaser! Ooh, did that hurt? Well if you've recognized your work and life choices come at the behest of others over yours, isn't it time NO was your new YES?

Relationships

You may have some beautiful people in your life, be it your partner, your football buddy, your sister or even Milo the cat. But how do they shape up against the work monster?

Which relationships have you neglected and why?
Sometimes that one last meeting that overran, the report that was due on Monday that ate into your weekend or the last-minute phone call at 8pm have a nasty way of gnawing at your relationships. People start to begrudge your lack of consistency or availability. You also get frustrated with their interruptions when you really just want to finish what you are doing in peace. 'So what if I missed Jonny's footie game, he plays every Sunday. I'll be there next week.'

The point is when we stop being inquisitive, open, aware and patient with our loved ones, these relationships start to weaken.

What stress do you absorb from work that is affecting other people in your life?
You may have become a bit of a whinge-bucket due to your love–hate relationship with work. Not everyone has the patience of a saint to put up with it and, in some cases, you may have rubbed a few people up the wrong way. You might think it's a solo journey you are on, but misery likes company and we can have a tendency to bring others down into the mire too when the going gets tough.

What activities, conversations and rituals need to be put in place to keep the love alive?
If you have found a few relationships that need a bit of TLC, now's the time to get started on fixing them even if it means having some difficult conversations. Some of these relationships will be the key scaffolding you need in your life to help you along, and they are even more essential when you are going through a transition like a career change.

Home

Do you have peace of mind in your home?
When you put the key in the door and walk in, does your heart sing or do you wish you could run back to the office? I've had those times when I wanted to be anywhere but home, so you end up staying out later and home just becomes somewhere you grab some shut-eye. If you don't have a place where you can draw a line between the office BS and your home/chill out zone, you need to fix this.

What is your wake-up or slow-down routine? Do you launch straight into action or fall into a heavy sleep? How can you change this?
Going back to my earlier point about migraines, aches and pains, when we don't take stock of how we start and end the day, all the stress just rolls into one big mass. We may think we are resting and nurturing ourselves but in reality we are just going through the motions. Eat. Drink. Sleep. Work. Repeat.

How can you create a space in your home to facilitate your wind-up and slow-down routine? Maybe you need a quiet spot to sit and have your coffee while you just take a moment to pause, a diffuser in your room to waft out some calming fragrances, a zone where you can go to be still before catching up with your partner or flatmates. The more you can create and set positive, clear and joyful habits around how you start and end your day, the better the day itself will become.

Work

Think of yourself as a pie. How big a slice of pie does work take? Do you begrudge it and how does that show?

Pick a pie visual. Maybe it's chicken, sweet potato or apple, whatever floats your boat. You had so many great intentions for what you were going to do with that pie, until one day you return to the kitchen and boom! A big juicy slice of that pie has been taken away and devoured.

How are you feeling about this? Pissed? Annoyed? Frustrated? This pie is your life, goddammit, and every day the job you hate is gorging on that pie, eating away at it and leaving you with crumbs. What are you gonna do about it?

What is your internal monologue? Is it filled with words like 'must', 'need' and 'have to'? How often do you say 'want to', 'can't wait to'?

I mean, this one is pretty simple really. If an average working day feels like a slog, it's time to bounce and thank God you bought this book.

Why should I bother with this?

I'd like to be cheeky and say 'because I say so' but that could come across as bossy and we are just getting to know each other. What I will say is that taking stock of where you sit across each of these areas is priceless. These four areas are all interwoven to create the beautiful, complex YOU. Continuous personal reflection and increased self-knowledge should be a non-negotiable act of service to ourselves *and to others*. If we are armed with the knowledge of what's working and what isn't in each of these facets of our lives, we can then take the *right* action and set some gutsy goals as opposed to guessing. Wandering around in the dark aimlessly wastes your time and keeps you in a constant vortex of indecision and pain. My hope is to empower you at each step of this journey with exercises to help you stay tuned to what you want.

After you've spent some time thinking about the four areas of your life (Self, Relationships, Home and Work), setting goals will become easier and they will take you closer to creating that work happiness you crave.

Goals, goals, goals. There's a big divide here between either setting yourself some big, audacious goals or setting the bar low so that you will easily exceed your expectations. I sit in the middle here.

The issue I have with setting low goals is that it keeps you playing small, with no challenges to build grit and resilience. On the flip side, when a goal is too big, we build up so much resistance to achieving it that we talk ourselves out of it. We put ourselves down for aiming too high when we miss the mark.

I want you to think for the moment about two goals: one you'd want to achieve if you knew you had magical superpowers and all the money and opportunities available in the world, and the minimum step you could take to give you some movement forwards.

Where feels like a happy middle point between these two? I'd rather you settle there as a start than just be blown from pillar to post with no goals whatsoever. We get into effective goal setting later on in Chapter 6, so sit tight.

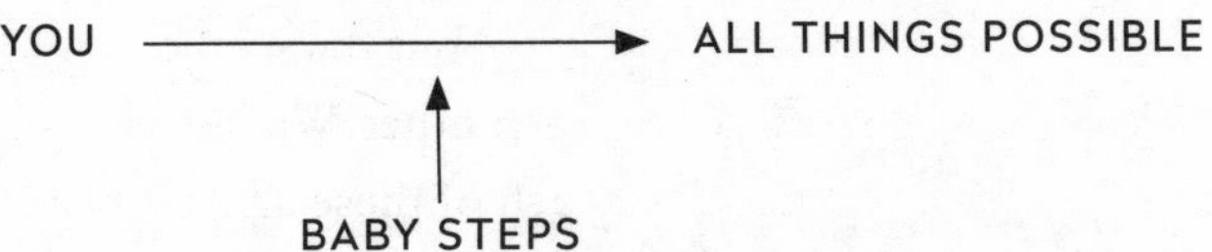

You might be thinking: Samantha, this is A LOT of self-reflection. As my old mate Socrates said, 'The unexamined life is not worth living.'

Reflective thinking can be uncomfortable. However, if you don't carve out time for reflection and that space to step back and see the wider picture, you won't mature or pick up any juicy knowledge that can help your success. Simple.

CHAPTER 2

REDEFINE THE BOUNDARIES

Work has elbowed itself into our play time and, in some cases, we are foregoing all play time to just work more. We've been putting our titles on a pedestal and, in the same breath, we've also set work a place at the dinner table, allowed it to get comfy on our memory-foam mattresses and eat into our downtime.

Technology has conveniently allowed us to become 'efficient' with our time (much to the detriment of our other needs) so that we can now:

- Answer emails on the work commute
- Gloss over your friend's crisis as you ponder whether that buzz on your phone is another email from your boss
- Check in with your colleagues in different time zones from your bed while your partner snoozes

Who is this person? This person is YOU!

I don't want you to think I'm making fun of you but, looking at the facts, we are seriously in love with our work and our phones which help us do more of it. Deloitte's Global Mobile Consumer Survey (Q4 2017) revealed that 34 per cent of us are checking our phones within 5 minutes of waking up and 48 per cent of us are responding to emails regularly between 2 and 3am. We've never been so 'wired'.

If you are ready to revolutionize your working life, then you've also got to do some spring cleaning around your boundaries. Where have you let some of them get soft? There are three ways in which we can either break or keep promises we make to ourselves and others. In life, we create not only physical boundaries but also psychological distance. Unfortunately, when it comes to work, we're bad at doing this.

Soft boundaries

Are you a little unsure of what should take priority, and so end up doing nothing or everything at work? You don't have a clue what your priorities or needs are, and you seem to just align yourself with what everyone else is doing. For example, when your colleagues are moaning about changes at work, do you join the chorus rather than figure out what the changes mean to you? Do you allow technology to run riot in your life and chart how you spend all your waking minutes?

It's a known fact that people lose confidence in others who wait for consensus, are slow to make decisions or just talk the talk. Stop making others read your mind and be clear about what you want and what you are willing to commit to. If you feel like your work is a dark cloud that you can't shift, perhaps you have to start making a more clear and decisive stand.

Rigid boundaries

Are you blinkered in your vision? Closed and walled off? This is also Mr/Ms Know It All at work, someone who is unwilling to take ideas or hear advice because they know best. You diminish what others have to say, arguing with everyone who does not agree with your point of view.

Your loved ones and co-workers can start to feel devalued, angry and insignificant. Your intellectual curiosity and creativity come to a halt when you stop looking at new ideas. To shift this boundary, ask yourself: 'What have I missed?' 'What am I not seeing?' 'How am I limiting new opportunities?'

Flexible boundaries

This is the sweet spot. This is where you consciously examine what is holding you back: what you are tolerating and why you are resigned to the idea that this is as good as it gets for you. You know when to take the initiative and when to ask for help.

Start to notice where your boundaries are floppy and how you can start to reinforce them when necessary to get you that extra pep in your step. This approach allows for progress, but at the same time gives you the strength to stand up against what doesn't suit you, sucks your time or harms your relationships.

I can go my own way... well, kinda

As you continue to discover more about what makes you click and your work-happiness aspirations, you may start to think you've got all the makings of a successful solo expedition. STOP!

While we can make significant progress on our own, having allies by our side can help us on this journey by:

- Invaluable cheerleading
- Helping us to question our challenges and find opportunities
- Acting as mirrors of behaviour we might need to develop, change or address

It's important to surround yourself with the right supporters for this mission. You may encounter tough critics along the way, namely in the form of yourself, and other not-so-helpful people on your mission.

Your voice of dissent

The messages I received about work when growing up were about hard graft, studying and working diligently in a job. There were always heavy discussions around why it wasn't the done thing to 'break the mould' and that entrepreneurship was dodgy. Often it's these voices of fear, worry, lack of knowledge and resistance that we internalize and they become our inner gremlin voices.

Welcome Dizzy – my gremlin. Sometimes it's a man and sometimes it's a woman. Dizzy likes to pop up just when I'm about to do something different that will make me shine (like write a book, for example), full of anecdotes about failure, painting visuals of people laughing at me to make me self-sabotage.

I named the gremlin not because I'm going mad, but because it helps me to identify my fears and understand what they are trying to tell me. By taking these simple steps, you can challenge your gremlins and boost your resilience, as opposed to letting them run you ragged.

Tune in to the stories you're telling yourself

Start listening to the stories you're telling yourself, particularly when you're feeling anxious, overwhelmed or upset, and notice the impact they have on you. Most of us are completely unaware of the potent effect these stories have on the way we feel and on our ability to act.

For example, when we say to ourselves:

- *'I'm not good enough.'* This generally makes us feel embarrassed, leaving us desperate to withdraw from the world around us.
- *'That's not fair.'* This makes us feel angry, causing us to blame others.
- *'I'm always stuffing things up. I can't seem to make it work.'* This often makes us feel guilty, sending us into a flurry of overcompensation.
- '*This is going to be bad.*' This makes us fearful and anxious.
- '*I'm such a loser.*' This generally makes us feel sad, lonely and grumpy.

These toxic belief systems are triggered when you face adversities, challenges or new experiences, namely making a career change, in an attempt to protect yourself from possible harm.

Ask yourself: is this story true?

You have to put your detective hat on and start hunting for what else might be happening. We are data-processing machines, but we can't analyse everything at once. Your brain can only process 40 bits of information per second every minute of every day so you are picking and choosing from the 11 million pieces of information your senses are receiving and what you have stored previously.

For example, you applied for a new job at a company you really admire and dream about working in, only to be rejected after the second round. It's easy to fall into the 'not being good enough' mindset, feeling defeated and dejected or decide 'it's not fair'. But then you are put forward for an alternative role with a sure path to success.

Our natural bias is towards correcting mistakes rather than recognizing what went well. We spend more time and give more weight to bad experiences and failures when what we really have to learn is how to focus on positive experiences.

To do this, we have to deliberately internalize positive experiences every day. Psychologist and neuroscientist Rick Hanson suggests in his book, *Hardwiring Happiness* (2013), that we can overwrite negative realities by linking them to the positive.

Try adopting the following:

- 'I didn't get that job, but I have a great shot at an alternative job'
- 'Now that I have a foot in the door, it may lead me to the job I want'
- 'It felt good walking around that company, I could be happy there even if the job isn't the right fit just yet'
- 'The team I will be working with are totally my kind of people'
- 'Maybe that job just wasn't what I actually needed'

To make your work happiness sustainable in moments of disappointment, you have to keep making the positive feelings stronger than the negative ones. The more you savour the positivity, the more you wire your brain to default to a happier reality.

Invest in the story that serves you best

Notice how what you're feeling and what you're willing to do changes as your story shifts. Which story serves you best in this situation for the outcomes that you want to achieve? Identifying which 'story' you tell yourself actually boosts your resilience and enables you to make more progressive changes. Keep asking yourself, what are the positives? What am I learning here that's beneficial for the new path I want to go down? Invest your energy and attention into this story and see what happens.

Other voices of dissent

Now that we've dealt with the internal voice of dissent, what about the people we live, play and work with? Any change you are going to make will attract some naysayers and non-believers. You will suddenly have a magnetic status and everyone will have an opinion as well as 'advice'.

'Every job is the same... they all suck!'
'Do you think you can possibly change industries at 42?'
'What will happen to the kids' school fees if you quit your job?'
'Why don't you just grin and bear it? Work isn't supposed to be fun!'

When any of these voices pop up, you need to think about your boundaries and decide where you stand. Reread the beginning of this chapter again if you need a refresher. In most cases, just stare at the naysayers, say thank you and stay focused. When it comes to thinking about mortgages/rent, time commitments to your partner, dependants and so on, it's important to have a sensible conversation about the risks, the possible fears and how you will overcome them. We often experience a tug of war with our head and heart through fear of other people's thoughts and worries. Later on, I cover how to plan a route that feels financially viable and navigate change without going bankrupt. My point is that money is often one of the biggest reasons we put up and shut up in jobs we aren't happy in, so it's worth looking at what compromises you are willing to make to get your work happiness. Communicate this, make a plan and then stick to it.

Not everyone is going to have your back. Fact! Remember that misery likes company. When you start to expand and spread your wings, grow and take on new challenges, you become a new person. You stand taller, your confidence levels rise. When others aren't able to do the same, they can sometimes start to feel small. With that comes nit-picking and naysaying. Sometimes your loved ones and friends just don't know how to help you, so can't support you in the way you need and may say things out of frustration. This might come out as harsh and abrasive, but it's just words. Build up your own little bubble for protection and visualize their words bouncing off you. Stay the course, I've got you covered.

SECTION 2:

WORKING OUT WHERE THE PAIN IS

CHAPTER 3

WHERE IS YOUR WORK HAPPINESS LURKING?

How do you want your work happiness to contribute to the person you want to become? Does your work represent the person you are today?

Previously we talked about job titles and the burden they place on our identities and life. As we've become obsessed with career ladders and titles, we've forgotten the missing piece in this puzzle here: YOU.

You've spent some time looking at where the work unhappiness is seeping into your relationships and perhaps your home and self-care. It's time to look forward and think:

- Who do I want to become in all of this?
- How will finding more work happiness help me get there?
- What does work happiness and success actually mean to me?
- How do I imagine spending my working days?

This is where some people struggle. It's definitely where I hit a stumbling block. I now want to rewind and give you some more context on how I navigated the see-saw of the success and happiness equation.

I graduated with my 2:1 Bachelor of Science (BSc) degree in Management and Marketing and smiley parents at graduation. They must have thought that I was all set now, so imagine their horror when

I limped wearily into and out of the advertising and branding world. This was success, wasn't it? Working in a series of grand advertising agencies working on 'big brands you see on TV'. What more could I want?

But I became sick of selling things I didn't believe in and being the go-between account manager. I wanted to be creative – an entrepreneur, a changemaker and be more transformational in my work. But how?

I just knew I deserved and could achieve more. The 'how' was the fuzzy part. So, in an effort to drown out the daytime work misery, I kept my soul alive with study in the evenings and weekends. Everything from fashion history to design and footwear – and I started to create my own semi-bespoke footwear fashion line. Big work bonuses that should have gone towards 'adulting' were spent going to Italian shoe fairs, buying in leather and heels, creating my sample collection and doing an apprenticeship in a shoe factory. So far so good... until we hit a recession. My financial backers dropped out, redundancy struck and the weight of funding a semi-bespoke footwear line played heavily on my mind and my bank balance.

Financial ruin was averted as I took a six-month maternity cover role at a retail trend and tech innovation agency. Helping to stimulate companies with new ideas, new strategies and product innovations, I was basically getting paid to dream up new ideas and source innovations globally. That's how it was sold to me. I was hoping that the multifaceted set of skills I had – my love of generating new ideas and passion for research and trends – would fly over those six months. Instead I was a nervous wreck, giving client presentations, forcing myself to love suggestions I didn't fully believe in (we couldn't be too radical after all).

The only joy was the chance to travel. Japan had always been on my hit list and here I was presenting to Sony in Tokyo, not once but twice! The happiness was fleeting though, I still felt empty and something still wasn't sticking. I spent evenings tackling my work profile and my skills. Post-it notes and highlighters helped me to dissect my melting pot of skills and experiences. From idea generation, branding, strategy, research, account management and tech to footwear and fashion design, I started to tease out the transferable elements, identifying how to sell them and align them with my vision to have more impact with people and deliver work I actually cared about.

People always commented on my sense of style and penchant for quirky shoes so I thought if I can't make them any more, I could at least source them for other people and help them find a style that sits right with them. So, after a training programme in professional personal styling and a short apprenticeship, I became a style therapist and personal brand educator. I helped professional women and entrepreneurs build their personal brands and style for success to find either work after redundancy, create the right look for their new self-employment or business venture, or just overcome their body and image gremlins that were standing in their way. Work flowed in from high-end clients in Dubai and Qatar wanting personal shopping, one-to-one programme clients from New York to Paris for online consultations and Skype clients in Australia and Switzerland for sessions on style and wardrobe detoxes.

While I was riding the wave of newfound career joys in my life, my body had other issues. I have a chronic blood disorder known as sickle-cell disease. It's a genetic condition where essentially my blood flow can become trapped in key joints around the body (mostly my knees, elbows and ankles), rendering me in excruciating pain and basically wiping me out, putting me in hospital on a morphine drip for days and then recuperating for weeks at home. It's been something in my life that I've never let hold me back from going after what I wanted, so much so that I became pretty good at masking painful attacks in my joints because I didn't want to call in sick to work. But there are other times where wandering off to take painkillers in the toilet was not enough and I found myself in a rough patch and on bed rest. It's easy to wallow with lots of time on your hands, but I decided it was time to hit the books and immerse myself in the world of psychology and behaviour change, signing up to take my coaching qualification when I felt better.

I'd found that as I discussed clothing and colours with my clients, they would share their work woes – everything from confidence issues, finding work that made them tick and worries about working for themselves. I was their work agony aunt and, in a weird way, I loved it. I started to see how the advice I gave them was helping them. The subtle changes my clients started to see in their confidence led them to invite me into their workplaces to speak about it. I was providing a cross between coaching, therapy, consulting and mindful styling with my own online resources.

By chance I saw an advert for a freelance lecturer at The School of Life – a global educational organization which offers classes and workshops on life issues. With my tapestry of skills, I was accepted and suddenly I found myself getting paid to give talks and design workshops around my portfolio career, the psychology of dress and how to find work that you love to a brand-new audience.

No two weeks were the same for me. Between coaching, delivering workshops and strategy consulting, I was having a ball. I started consulting for a remote-working tech company, because the tech industry had always appealed to me and it was an opportunity I wasn't going to pass up. Still in its infancy, with just seven people on the team, this company had no HR/People/Culture person and major plans to grow quickly. With a knack for spotting problems and identifying how to pitch myself, I brazenly put together a proposal to become their Head of Happiness, helping them to identify how to create a remote-working culture, take the time to get to know their global teams and shape their vision for a happy workforce. They loved it. The tech geek in me loved it too and so my happiness began to soar. I spent over two years there, took some more training in systems change and group dynamics coaching before branching out on my own as a Happiness Consultant.

My journey wasn't all sweet-smelling roses, of course. There were many moments of WTF nestled in with joy, luck, pure delight and a large amount of bloody hard work.

So what are the morals of this little sweet tale?

1. We can all be work-happiness revolutionaries if we identify how we want our lives and work to shape us as people.
2. Be willing to consistently dissect your skills, strengths, weaknesses and the value you can provide.
3. Openly leverage any opportunities that come your way.
4. Test different concepts and journeys.
5. Keep learning about yourself and other people, and build your network along the way.
6. Be open to the twists and turns and never give up.
7. Don't let your past career define or limit your next career.

Isn't it time 'success' and 'work happiness' became a couple?

What does success look like to you? Is it:

- Spending your weekends in Lisbon and weekdays working in an agency in London?
- Living on your eco farm, selling your home-grown produce locally and consulting others on how to do it?
- Making partner at your firm and living in that fantastic house in the postcode of your dreams?
- Working intensely in a contract role for six months and then taking six months off just to learn a new skill or write a novel?
- Homeschooling your kids and working remotely?
- Working for an innovation hub where your working days are spent just brainstorming new ideas and nothing else?

These are just a handful of ways in which past clients are crafting their own versions of success and work happiness.

Success and work happiness never used to be good bedfellows in the past. They were always at odds with each other. 'Success' used to be super lofty, set in its ways and out of reach while 'work happiness' was considered the 'nice-to-have-but-poor-substitute' date, the one you should be going on but never really made a priority. But times are changing and, with a little bit of creativity, these two can work well together.

It's time to break free from the mould and ask yourself some more tough questions. Yes, I know I'm cracking the whip a bit, but I want you to stop standing in your own way and unleash what you've kept hidden.

EXERCISE

Career daydreams

Grab a pen and let's go.

- If all jobs paid your dream monthly income, what would you really like to do? (What ideas have you been holding back on due to money concerns?)
- If you could speak to your 16-year-old self and offer some work-happiness advice, what would you say?

Take a moment to look at your current situation and consider what is constricting your creative thinking around:

- How you currently work.
- Why you continue to work in the way you do.
- What you think you can't change.

What is the success and work happiness you actually want now, as opposed to what you've been conditioned to think?

Are you choosing to stay small because it's easy? OUCH! That's harsh I know, but while getting comfortable with discomfort isn't our favourite thing, it's a really good skill. This is one of those moments where you need to stretch, challenge and push yourself for the change you want.

Being an agent of change: what will I need to stretch to get there?

It's no longer OK for you to lean back and let work happen to you or for it to just be a place you show up at between 9am and 6pm.

In order to find work happiness, you need to become entrepreneurial in your quest. The word 'entrepreneur' has been paraded about as the best alternative to working full time for someone else or in a job you hate. It's been glorified as the best way to achieve your dreams, but I don't believe it works for all. Later we will look at how the application of the signature personality traits of entrepreneurship can drive forward your work happiness (see Chapter 6, page 99).

The path that leads us to the modern-day work environment is one that is stultified, narrow, predetermined and just dampens our spirits. Realistically, school didn't set me up for success. Maybe yours did. I'm so jealous. However, I'm guessing you had a traditional school path where days blurred into one another with a mix of set classes, routines, unhappy teachers and delusional career advisors. This rote learning and spoon-fed curriculum creates docile individuals who become afraid of colouring outside of the lines.

What does this look like? Well, we put up with things because we don't believe we have any right to make changes. We don't find it easy to challenge the status quo for fear of rocking the boat, believing that those with more senior titles than us know best. Schools don't set out with the intention of creating entrepreneurs, they are focused on creating workers needed to keep companies going. So, it's going to take some shapeshifting from you to move beyond this to reach 'happy' status.

From what I've seen, many people approach career change with a fixed and fearful, unplanned and scatty mentality.

'I can't throw away all my years as…'

'I've been a successful X for ten years, I don't have what it takes to become good at Y as well.'

'I'm 45 with a mortgage and three kids, I'm too old and I don't have time to start from scratch.'

It's easy to let your past career journey define or limit your next career chapter. But how does that help you? Nobody said career change was a straight path with a neat ending. No, this is not going to be easy, but if something is worth doing, you have to put your back into it, right? We have to be open to the twists, turns, the steps back to take leaps forward and the umpteen trials and tribulations we may face.

The signature four steps to work happiness

To get this career thing locked down and successful, you've got to have a plan. It sounds exciting to turn up to work and savour the moment when you hand in your resignation and quit. And then what? The shaky moments of terror when cash gets low and the incessant questions from loved ones about what you're doing with your life start driving you mad. Career change isn't like some IKEA furniture that you can knock up without looking at the instructions. You might be able to deal with a slightly wonky drawer for a while, but a wonky career change has deeper ripple effects. Take the smart road to get the right answers.

1. Pick the right change

There's nothing worse than not knowing why you want to revolt. Moaning for moaning's sake about the drudgery of your work is useless unless you are willing to investigate what you need and want to change. Creating a foundation and understanding your values, current position, interests and career-future vision is core to achieving your work happiness.

You've got to do the excavation first to build the house foundations. You don't get to the decorating stage without any walls or floors. As you do the digging, you are going to discover some patterns around your work. Have you always been proactive in seeking change at work? Do you grab the opportunities that come by chance or through your network of friends and contacts? These patterns are markers for what to build next and where you need to strengthen your foundations.

2. Evaluate your toolkit

Finding work happiness isn't about scrapping all your previous work skills and experience and starting from scratch. This is where people yearn for the quick fixes, but the patience to evaluate your skills and strengths will yield massive dividends.

This step is more curation than creation. Auditing over destroying. Connecting the dots and weaving together your skills and capabilities. Identifying your signature blend of skills and strengths will give you the power to know what you have to offer, how you want to work and how to sell what you have.

3. Take action

Start with mini experiments to dip your toe in the water of your new direction. This will help you build bridges between where you are now and where you want to go.

Later in the book we are going to look in more detail at the various types of action for each of the two routes – Love It or Leave It. And no, I'm not just going to say follow your passion or find your purpose. You should know me better by now. While I do want you to follow your groove AND do what you actually give a sh*t about doing, you need a strategy, direction and method. Career transition is a winding road. But nobody said I couldn't give you a map and some 'food' for the journey. There's no need for aimless ambling.

4. Keep momentum

This is all about maintaining commitment and drive to forge ahead in a new direction. It's easy to start off with great energy, but the engine will soon run out of fuel if you don't top it up. I know this for a fact and the last thing you want is to break down without any backup. When you are part of a revolution, the journey can be relentless, so you have to be prepared to keep up your stamina.

I wouldn't be a great coach if I didn't prepare you with tools on how to boost your resilience to overcome obstacles, manage stress, silence your inner gremlin voices and build the skills and support systems to keep you going. But it's not about dipping in and out of these stages – I've created them in this way because when you follow the plan, it works.

As we prepare to find your work happiness, I thought I'd end with some brilliant words from Alain de Botton at The School of Life. He offered this thought to help us on our work-happiness journey:

'The best kind of work is the work we'd do even if it didn't pay, even if it wasn't a job. The best jobs approximate the condition of a hobby with the added benefit of a salary. This is an extremely rare prospect, but a hugely beautiful one.'

Alain de Botton

It's my hope and number one wish on our adventure together that the prospect of work happiness isn't a rare and alien one for you but a beautiful, tangible reality.

The next chapter will help you focus on where the pain currently sits in your working life so you can start to remove that thorn in your side. Let's go!

CHAPTER 4

PICK THE RIGHT CHANGE

Where is the PAINNNNNNN?

Most people don't really know what the pain is when it comes to their work or career. They just know that something isn't right and they want out immediately. You need to get to the root of the problem versus just numbing it with after-work drinks. When we make big career leaps without proper insights, we often end up back to square one. Stuck in a job that might pay more but is a new kind of hell.

When I sit down with clients, either one-to-one or in a workshop, the first question I ask is 'Where is the pain?'.

They look at me blankly for a bit, maybe responding:

'All of it, I'm just tired…'

'I don't know, maybe it's the people…'

'I can't be sure I ever loved my job…'

All of this is a good start because it helps to create the landscape for further exploration.

Then I invite them to decipher whether it's the PEOPLE, INDUSTRY/SECTOR or JOB that's causing the pain.

Light bulbs start to go off as if this simple clarification has lifted the fog and then I often hear:

'Oh, actually I love my team, but the work isn't inspiring.'

'I don't think I ever loved law. I fell into it because my parents are lawyers.'

'It's my boss, he/she is a nightmare…'

'I want to be more creative in my role.' (This is the statement I hear most frequently.)

By first deciphering where the change needs to take place, we can then dive into what degree of change is needed. Most people get caught in the headlights with career change because they think it's about a massive upheaval. Through a variety of exercises, this chapter will help you to understand the type of career change you want and how to go for it in a way that works for you, your circumstances and desires.

I know there is a temptation to shy away from the exercises or see them as a bit time-consuming, but you need to lay the foundations now or live in a shaky house later.

People

'For me, the role isn't the issue, it's some of the people in my office. They are extremely blunt and not willing to see the bigger picture on ideas. I feel like I get push back on every small detail.'

A one-to-one client

Working in a company is much like being part of a wild, jungle habitat. Everyone and everything has a role to play and, as much as we think we are independent, there is a wider and sometimes invisible interdependence that can impact our output, behaviours and attitudes.

Work can be the place where you form lifelong friendships, meet your partner or even find the co-founder of your new business. Gallup reports that 30 per cent of employees have a best friend at work. When we are lucky enough to have one, we have fun, and dealing with customers feels like a joy, not a chore. We speed through tasks with pace and generally feel great about ourselves. However, if you find yourself in the 'no-friends zone' you have just a 1 in 12 chance of being attuned and committed to your work, according to Gallup. That sucks.

While belonging and connecting is high up there in the happiness and productivity stakes, sometimes it comes with problems. Competition for roles and titles adds disruption to your workflow, and a lack of trust elsewhere counteracts those joyous water-cooler moments and after-work hangouts with Anoushka on floor two. Add to this the mix of toxic personalities from leaders, managers or co-workers, who will rub you the wrong way, pick holes in your very existence and make you wonder why you got out of bed today. You slowly start to believe that working somewhere else would be a better idea. This is the 'itch to jump' that I was talking about earlier.

It's easy to say that your colleagues should be the ones to change and allow you to just continue in peace on the road to greatness. But when people wind us up, it highlights something we need to *change, welcome or address in our own behaviour.* Sorry to be a Debby Downer here but I've had a few trolls in my time, so I am speaking from experience. The truth is that it's up to us how much we let them trigger us and what we will do about it. Equally we need to be clear about who helps us to flourish and pushes us to be better, and how we can manage the people that hamper our progress. Taking into account that you are not working in a vacuum, it's best to arm yourself with the knowledge to make some real changes.

Below are the four key character traits that exist in an office.

Commander

- **Attributes:** self-confidence, directness, forcefulness, risk-taking.
- **Driven by:** power and authority, competition, winning, success.
- **Hates:** loss of control, being taken advantage of, vulnerability.
- **Ripple effect on others:** lack of concern for others, impatience, insensitivity.
- **When communicating with them:** be specific, provide facts and avoid generalization, focus on solutions over problems and be succinct.
- **What to watch out for:** they will expect a lot from themselves and you. This comes across by incessant poking of holes at your ideas, approach or suggestions because they want to explore the best method.

  They have little patience for anything that stands in the way of them achieving success.

Navigator

- **Attributes:** sociable, optimistic, talkative, enthusiastic.
- **Driven by:** group activities, relationships, social recognition.
- **Hates:** loss of influence, being ignored or rejected, disapproval.
- **Ripple effect on others:** lack of follow-through, disorganization, impulsiveness.
- **When communicating with them:** get discursive and personable, allow them to be curious about you and invite discussion. They will snooze with too much detail – and don't talk over them, that's a no-no.
- **What to watch out for:** Making decisions off the cuff. It's all a bit of a whirlwind with these people. Sometimes you don't know if you are coming or going. They value enthusiasm and want to get going without much consideration for the organization or the smaller details needed to action ideas.

Pacifier

- **Attributes:** calm, modest, patient, team player, great listening abilities.
- **Driven by:** stable environments, unified visions, opportunities to help, being appreciated.
- **Hates:** offending others, rapid change.
- **Ripple effect on others:** indecisive, appears to be a walkover, set in their ways.
- **When communicating with them:** express an interest in them, provide answers to their questions in a clear manner. Politeness goes a long way.
- **What to watch out for:** they hold their tongue a lot, allowing most people to become sceptical of their true motivations. People love their analytical and precise working methods, and their efficacy, but they sometimes jar others with their inflexibility and inability to speak up and initiate change.

Cautious

- **Attributes:** sceptical, reserved, quiet.
- **Driven by:** opportunities to use expertise and pick up new skills, attention to quality and detail.
- **Hates:** slapdash work, criticism, being accused or finding out they are in the wrong.
- **Ripple effect on others:** can overanalyse and be critical of others and their actions, can isolate themselves from others.
- **When communicating with them:** lose the emotional language and keep strictly to the facts. They haven't got time for 'I feel' statements. Be patient with them.
- **What to watch out for:** under pressure they can retreat and become hesitant about next steps especially if it doesn't align with their orderly framework. They struggle to see other people's insights or emotions and hate lack of control. Cooperation is low on their agenda.

Take a look at the profiles above and work out which profile applies to you and which factors seem to be causing you the most hassle on a day-to-day basis. This is especially helpful if you think people are the cause of your work misery. To find out which office character you fall into, try the quiz on page 231. Or maybe you already know…?

I wonder if you can guess where I sit? Not surprisingly, I'm a Navigator with Pacifier a close second and Cautious following after.

Now I want you to think about the difficult relationships you might be navigating at work – maybe it's your teammate who is a little wishy-washy and this irks your driven nature. Perhaps your boss wants to get buy-in from everyone around the table against making a stand once in a while. Or perhaps your assistant requires a bit more handholding than you have patience for when time pressures get tight. These everyday scenarios can build up and have us feeling conflicted, thwarted and disheartened.

In Chapter 7 we are going to look at how to tackle those tricky colleagues whatever their personality type and hopefully move you from feeling pissed off to being a smooth operator. But next, let's dip into a quick exercise.

EXERCISE

Work memory lane

Think about the last 3–5 years of your working history. It doesn't matter if you've been in the same job, had multiple experiences or quit to start your own company. I want you to reflect on the types of people you seem to buck up against the most and which people might be your triggers.

- What interactions did you find most enjoyable and energizing?
- What interactions did you find the most negative or frustrating?

These could be anything from meetings, water-cooler moments, client sessions, networking, work socials and so on.

- Which type of person are you drawn to working with?

This exercise is useful to help you comprehend which types of people you get on with successfully and which ones make your working experience the least pleasurable. Like I said before, work is a jungle and it's important that you learn whom you play well with, which people to stay away from and who are your best allies or supporters.

If you've realized you always seem to gravitate towards and already work with fabulous people, lucky you! If not, I'm sorry mate. But, on the flip side, I'm going to share with you ways to tackle this in Chapter 7.

Next up we investigate another heavyweight area of 'pain': industry and sector. Maybe you can relate here?

Industry/sector

> *'I really like my job as a software architect. I spend my days making decisions and finding solutions to problems. But you've helped me realize where my pain is. I just don't care enough about my company's service or product. What should I do?'*
>
> **Client, tech industry**

One of the biggest killers of work joy is knowing that you love what you do but feeling that the values, mentality and direction of your company and/ or industry are at odds with what you want. Every day feels like a drag because you are literally fighting with yourself and your values. The only thing that softens the blow might be that you may have a great team, so this can help the hours fly by. But that's if you are lucky!

This is exactly how I felt when I worked in digital advertising. If I had to think of another solution to get women to eat more diet cereal or another interactive online game for a sugary children's cereal, I would have screamed. I loved connecting with my colleagues, but I couldn't bring myself to feel cheery about selling people unhealthy crap.

I've coached numerous individuals who once loved the public sector but have become worn down by limited budgets and poor self-care, and I've helped those looking to leave the corporate private sector or a particular industry for more sustainable and altruistic opportunities.

At last count, there are over 24 different types of industries you could find yourself in from law, pharmaceuticals and hospitality to finance, aerospace and defence. You get my drift. That's just at the time of writing. While this might be exciting, it can equally be paralysing as the thought of the possible time and expense of retraining to fit into another sector can keep us in a state of permanent indecision.

The key thing to hold on to here is that whatever your area of expertise, there will always be elements that you can carry over that could be beneficial in another industry. While some industries might be contracting, others within the social and technological realms are going through stratospheric change, development and innovation. You may be thinking, '*That sounds exciting Samantha! But, let's be realistic, I can't do that.*'

Why do we get tunnel vision on how we can progress?
I think for the most part individuals can get caught in the flux of change, overtaken by fear that we don't know enough about new sectors to even give it a go. It all just leaves us stuck. Never underestimate what you have to offer that can be attractive to another industry going through prolific change; the best innovations and change always come from those with fresh eyes and new perspectives. Either way, it's about moving beyond a rigid sense of where you can find happiness and exploring options in unknown places.

Let's strip it right back.

EXERCISE

The B.R.I.D.G.E. – Part 1

This exercise will help you move beyond feeling stuck to getting the knowledge you need to take action. It just takes a little reflection time. Grab your notebook and let's investigate.

Belief: In which area do you have little faith or belief in your current company? The product, service, leadership style or company culture? And why?

Results: What does success look like to you? Are you after your boss's job or not? Are you motivated by awards? Can you achieve success in your current industry/sector?

Impact: What valuable knowledge or insight do you want to share? What's the biggest impact you want to make? What will be your legacy? Can you achieve it in your current industry/sector?

Desires: What do you desire more of?

- More money
- R.E.S.P.E.C.T. baby
- Status and superiority
- Steady times and stability
- Work that makes your heart swell
- Work and life harmony

Growth: Is your industry growing or shrinking? What are your prospects for finding a new job in a similar space? Is your place of work in a tricky financial position?

Enrich: How does your day-to-day experience make you feel? Do you feel competent, happy and enriched, or unsuccessful, challenged, exhausted and bored? What are you absorbing and learning?

From this you should start to glean some insights, such as:

The company culture sucks and my industry isn't known for winning best workplace of the year awards, so change is gonna be slow.

Perhaps you want more money and recognition for all the skills you have, but you don't want to sell your soul to the workplace devil to get it.

The product or service the company is selling may feel a bit superficial and trend-orientated and you'd rather be working on something more sustainable or related to real-world issues.

The industry might be known for its late nights and soul-sapping pace and actually all you want is to be able to see your kids before they go to bed.

Armed with this knowledge, your next step is to discover what other industry opportunities exist. However, not everything that glitters is gold.

For instance:

- Moving from a big behemoth organization to a start-up in a new industry is going to have its drawbacks – perhaps a pay drop, less security and you may be expected to wear many hats
- Maybe a change in industry might require a little training. Are you OK with that?
- Reaching out to people you've never met before to build relationships and bolster new connections might not fill you with glee

Oh, the harsh truths! Life is all about a little give and take. Keep in mind what you are prepared to compromise on to help ease the pain.

You've got the willpower and courage. You've bought this book, so you are ready to make this happen. Don't feel defeated just yet. Later on, we are going to tackle how to jump from one industry to another and how to start conversations about your work happiness and desires with people who can help you make the leap!

EXERCISE

The B.R.I.D.G.E. – Part 2

Choose three industries from the list below that pique your interest. You may equally just have one or two, that's fine. I want you to take some of your early **B.R.I.D.G.E.** ideas (see pages 39–40) and see how they fit with some of the industries you are curious about.

Explore all the possible opportunities that exist for you within each industry. These might be career or business ideas you might develop that use the skills you currently have.

If you want to brainstorm other job role opportunities or horizontal shifts in your current industry/sector, that's cool too.

Industries

Administration and Support Services
Advertising, Marketing and Public Relations
Aerospace and Defence
Agriculture
Arts and Culture
Consulting
Educational Institutions
Energy and Natural Resources
Engineering, Construction and Infrastructure
Estate Agent
Financial Services
Food and Beverage
Government
Healthcare
Hospitality
Human Resources
Law
Manufacturing
Media
Pharmaceuticals
Professional Services
Retail and Consumer Goods
Sports
Technology
Telecommunications
Transportation
Travel

Unearthing your industry desires

I want you to get visual and start to think about the moves you are keen to make. It's easy to get stuck in our heads with this decision-making process but it pays to map things out on paper to give yourself a clearer view. Dissecting an industry down into the small building blocks that intrigue you can help you start to see how pieces of the puzzle can come together.

Here are a few examples to get the juices flowing:

- You could bring your financial acumen from a small accountancy firm to a new start-up company that is working on a disruptive mobile banking offering
- Or use your sales skills honed in a pharmaceuticals company to help an independent solar panel producer find new audiences and markets to manufacture and sell their groundbreaking designs
- Maybe you are a medical researcher ready to move from working inside a lab in a hospital or university to using your research skills for a robotics company keen to develop robotic arms that can support stroke or Alzheimer patients who have lost the use of their limbs
- A freelance arts and culture consultant used to creating projects around art and music geared towards inspiring the youth could move into the public sector and use your knowledge working with young teens and adults to become a governmental policy advisor on how best to create more creative curricula in schools

But wait! I can hear your fear monsters

'I don't know anything about other industries.'

'I've been a lawyer for ages. Anything else seems really alien to me.'

Stick with me. This is a list of industries that you would attempt to work in if you knew you couldn't fail and money, time and other demands weren't a factor.

EXERCISE

The B.R.I.D.G.E. – Part 3

Work through each of your new industry choices and, following the B.R.I.D.G.E. structure, answer the questions that resonate in each section below:

Belief: What is the ethos of the company or organization in this new industry that feels like a better fit for you?

Results: Can you achieve the type of success you are looking for in this industry/sector? Can you see the road to a senior position clearly mapped out? Is it something you'd like for yourself perhaps? Do you want to work where there is no hierarchy and everyone has a say in how decisions are made successfully?

Impact: What's the biggest impact you want to make? Is it focused on a small community, industry-wide or global?

Desires: Some people love the idea of making a lot of money in banking and the financial tech industry, but others feel it's too soulless and cutthroat. One person's trash is another's treasure. Does this new industry meet your desires?

Growth: How can you research where this new industry might be going? How many people on average apply for jobs? Is this an industry facing constant disruption or is it slow to change?

Enrich: How can you learn about the inner workings of the office environment? Play detective and find out from your network of friends, family, old co-workers or ex-employees, industry forums and social media what the culture is like. Are you suitably qualified? Will it stretch you to learn new things?

If you want to go beyond your notebook, find a blank wall and use Post-it notes to help you tease out elements you want to learn more about.

EXERCISE

The B.R.I.D.G.E. – Part 4

Take a step back and look at your potential options.

- Which of your two or three chosen industries ranks the highest out of ten in terms of interest and excitement? Why?
- Are you able to identify any common themes? If so, what are they?
- Where are the glaring differences in your choices? Perhaps you want to work in a fashion start-up because you like the freedom to innovate and get creative but equally you value making a big salary in the finance sector.

Taking your top choice, I want you to make a list of places where you can find 20 people who might be in that industry, that you can reach out to either via email to set up a call or a coffee date. This is what I call a 'career fire-starter' conversation. We go deeper into this in Chapter 9, so hang tight!

Trust me, you have to get out there and start talking to people. You need to identify what the day-to-day working reality is like. Daydreaming and fantasizing is not allowed and it won't stop the pain either.

What I want you to do is to get comfortable visualizing what your alternate 'possible self' could be. What do I mean by this? Hermina Ibarra, an Organizational Behaviour professor at INSEAD and Harvard business schools and author of *Working Identity: Unconventional Strategies for Reinventing Your Career* (2003), suggests that career change involves discovering and stepping into the many versions of ourselves we might like to be but haven't yet become.

Maybe you've always dreamed of being a criminal investigator or writing a short film that is shown at Cannes Film Festival. Don't sell yourself short; it's all about seizing that vision and making a map to follow.

The job

> *'Arghh, every day it's the same: firefighting and endless meetings. I come alive creating designs and visualizing solutions but the opportunity to be creative dwindles as my week progresses.'*
>
> **Client, fashion industry**

We've talked about two possible pain points that could be stamping out your work joy. Now it's time to look at the third: the day-to-day job itself.

So what is it about the job itself that really drives you mad? Often we can keep ourselves confined in a role that no longer fits us because we let our inner gremlins take over. The only way to know what we are really drawn to doing is to shine a light on it.

I want to find out which particular tasks leave you flatlining and which ones get your heart racing.

EXERCISE

The job 'heart' check

During one week, list all the tasks in your role and note which leave you:

Flatlining: boring tasks that leave you frustrated

Warming up: tasks that pique your interest

Heart racing: actions and tasks that get you feeling energized

Use the following questions to help guide your answers:

- ➤ What work activities bore you and leave you staring at the clock?
- ➤ What's the most aggravating element about your daily work?
- ➤ What do you most look forward to on your to-do list each week?
- ➤ If you fast forward your life into the future, what elements would you be most proud of in your current day-to-day work?

For example:

Flatlining	Warming up	Heart racing
Administrative tasks, writing meeting agendas.	Holding creative development sessions for a new product.	Facilitating a workshop, closing a sale.

What did you learn from this exercise?

By doing this exercise, you will begin to see what really annoys you. You may also see inklings of where you aren't being stretched and how much of the heart-racing stuff you are actually doing over the course of a week.

Just what the doctor ordered

Well, you've come to the end of this examination of your current work status. With these exercises, you are slowly becoming your own work-happiness doctor. It's time to see what might be the right diagnosis for your malaise with one last exercise.

EXERCISE

The job prescription

Now it's time to prescribe yourself the right medicine. I want you to fill out this prescription form which outlines what steps you need to take to steer clear of the pain you want to avoid. This is your opportunity to make a clear commitment to yourself and look after your work-happiness future.

I've made a start on what your potential medication ideas could be below.

Name:..

D.O.B:..

Address:..

Medication name	Reason for medication
To work with people who are creative.	I come alive when I get to generate ideas with others and create new projects.
To work in a start-up or scale-up that is growing quickly.	I like an environment that is fast-paced, spontaneous and allows me to use different skills or wear many hats.
To find work that allows me to manage large teams.	It's important to me to work with lots of unique characters towards a common goal. I have great people skills and I've also been told I'd be a good manager.

Patient is required to start treatment, effective immediately.

Signed:

....

When the pain becomes too much

I remember when I was a little girl watching my mum struggling to finish her breakfast in the morning. She looked like she hadn't slept and would drag her feet when normally she'd be telling me to get a move on to school. I was puzzled, wondering what was going on. She would cry into her porridge and nothing I'd say made a difference. One evening, I decided to eavesdrop on my parents as they discussed her *work situation*. Really? I thought someone had died! I wondered how work could be this grim. I mean, school was pretty intense, so I thought it couldn't be worse than that but evidently it was. Mum sobbed as she talked about her boss, how she wanted voluntary redundancy but was aware that school fees and the mortgage weren't going to pay themselves. Slowly, over a series of evenings, my parents planned mum's escape route and the sacrifices they would need to make until she found alternative work.

That was my earliest experience of how work could crush a strong spirit. I grew up with that vision in my head, hoping to avoid that until I found myself milling over my oats in the morning, dragging my heels and pouring my heart out over happy-hour cocktails with my girls. I shrunk every time I entered the office and found myself daydreaming of better solutions at my desk and during meetings.

How do you feel at work? Are you fed up with office politics and bitching? Are you tired, weary and fatigued? You are not alone. In the UK alone, 15.4 million working days, or 57 per cent, were lost in 2017/18 due to work-related stress, depression or anxiety. Stress, depression or anxiety accounted for 44 per cent of all work-related cases of ill health.

The distressing thing is that stories like my mum's are not dissimilar to the work-induced anxieties that I hear from my clients. This is not OK! Below are some of the reasons I hear:

- *'I feel overworked and underpaid.'* Like a hamster on a treadmill, there's more work, unrealistic expectations and no opportunities for growth. On top of this, you're just about making ends meet every month.
- *'I feel like from the moment I wake up, I'm either on my phone or stuck in front of my computer. I'm expected to be on call all the time.'* The blurred

lines between work and play caused by tech make it more difficult to stop thinking about work when you aren't at work.

- *'We are stretched in my department. I'm doing three different roles and I'm exhausted.'* In times of economic instability and uncertainty, companies start to tighten their belts which means people are stretched thinly. Equally, in a start-up where resources are tight, you may be stuck doing more than you bargained for which can add to your stress levels.
- *'My boss drives me insane. I feel micromanaged and frustrated' and/or 'My boss never notices when I do a good job.'* Feeling underappreciated by your boss or your team can have a huge impact on day-to-day work life, decreasing your happiness levels.

Stress can have good consequences; it can be the trigger we need to push ourselves to excel. Or it can halt us in our tracks, wear us down and make us susceptible to burn out.

What happens when we get stressed at work?

Stress manifests in several ways. Which of the following do you recognize?

COGNITIVE SYMPTOMS

- Memory problems
- Trouble pulling your thoughts together
- Anxious, racing thoughts
- Anticipating the worst at all times

EMOTIONAL SYMPTOMS

- Snappy temper
- Constant state of overwhelm
- Feeling lonely or isolated
- Depression

PHYSICAL SYMPTOMS

- Muscle tension and tightness
- Frequent colds and sickness
- Headache, shoulder and back pain
- Low sex drive

BEHAVIOURAL SYMPTOMS

- ➤ Increased use of alcohol/drugs/cigarettes to relieve stress
- ➤ Nervous habits such as nail biting, teeth grinding or pacing
- ➤ Over- or undereating
- ➤ Excesses in terms of exercising, spending

So how do we combat this stress? There are four ways I'd suggest of doing this:

1. Knowing you are stressed is the first half of the battle. It takes a lot of confidence to take a step back and be real with yourself that you are in dire straits and need help. Your willingness to be vulnerable around this is key to moving forward and achieving the change and success you seek.

2. Working your way through this book. I would say that, wouldn't I? But it's true, you bought it for a reason – because you are tired of your current milieu and want to do something about it. This is a positive step towards releasing all that fraught job tension and stress.

3. There is so much magic in speaking to someone who is out of your social circle/system to help you manage and process what's happening to you mentally and/or physically. That may be a therapist or counsellor – I love my weekly sessions with my therapist to offload, dissect and rejig perspectives. If going to visit a therapist feels out of your budget right now, there are cheaper online diary therapy services for a fraction of the price or you could create your own personal support and accountability group to navigate your work-happiness evolutions.

4. Turn your self-care up a notch. When all hell breaks loose on the work front, it's easy for our self-care to nosedive too. The following exercise is about assessing your self-care across each of the four areas I mentioned earlier. It is not exhaustive, but merely suggestive. You can also add areas of self-care that are relevant for you. Please rate yourself on how often and how well you are taking care of yourself. When you are finished, look for patterns in your responses:

- Are you more active in some areas but ignore others? Are there items on the list that make you think, 'I would never do that'?
- Listen to:
  - Your inner responses
  - Your internal dialogue
  - How you make yourself and your happiness a priority while you are in the work tornado

To get you started on the road to better self-care, take a look at the Nourishment Diary overleaf.

EXERCISE

Nourishment diary

Cast your eye over the list below and keep a nourishment diary for a couple of weeks. Pick at least two activities from each section that you will attempt to do in order to nurture and nourish yourself during the ups and downs of your stressful job to soothe the pain you are feeling.

Self

- Eat regularly and eat healthy, nutritious meals. Be mindful of what foods zap your energy
- Exercise – a short burst of activity for a minimum of 30 minutes a day. This could be a brisk walk, a yoga class or a stint at the gym
- Notice what's happening on the inside. Do a temperature check on yourself. Is it a warm sunny day or stormy and dark? What are your current thoughts, beliefs, attitudes, feelings?
- Get a massage to move energy and blood flow through your body maybe once a month or every quarter
- Take time to be sexual – with yourself, with a partner
- Say no to extra responsibilities that don't feel right
- Engage your intelligence in a new area – go to an art show, sports event or the theatre

Relationships

- Schedule regular dates with your partner or spouse
- If you have children, schedule regular activities with them, from reading them a bedtime story to visiting a museum or a game of basketball
- Spend time with others whose company you enjoy
- Call, check on or see relatives
- Spend time with pets
- Stay in contact with faraway friends
- Don't be afraid to ask for help if you need it. It's a sign of strength to know what you need and how to ask for it
- Enlarge your social circle
- Ask for help when you need it
- Share a fear, hope or secret with someone you trust

Home

- Create an inspiring space that's filled with your favourite books, art from your travels and quotes and things that make you laugh or motivate you
- Identify comforting spaces and places in your home that help you relax and unwind that have certain fabrics, furniture and soft furnishings
- Design your bedroom to be a place that supports a good night's sleep, 'fun times' and a marked distance away from the world of work
- Monitor and alter phone habits to help you take mini detoxes or breaks from technology when needed
- Change your light bulbs to softer, energy-efficient ones
- Install time-management software on your computer to boost your productivity instead of endless online surfing if you work from home

Work

- Take a break during the work day (at lunch, for example)
- Take time to chat with co-workers
- Make quiet time to complete tasks
- Identify projects or tasks that are exciting and rewarding.
- Set limits or boundaries with clients and colleagues
- Balance your workload so that no one day or part of a day is 'too much'.
- Tap into a peer support or mentor group weekly or monthly to provide regular guidance and insights on your growth

This is not an exhaustive list, so feel free to add or change to suit you.

I am ready to be pain-free!

Where is the pain for you?

'It's the people, it's all so clear now!'

'Whoop, I'm ready to move into a new industry. Now's the time!'

'Err… Samantha… it hurts everywhere!'

Some of you might have been triggered with sparks of insight and action. The rest of you might still be scratching your head, frozen by a deluge of thoughts or realizations. That's fine.

Together, the exercises that you've just completed will become part of a bigger puzzle which I'm piecing together for you. Slowly but surely the complete picture will be revealed and you can start to make some choices.

Next, we'll be assessing your strengths, skills, passions and motivations. It's time to tease out these beauties so that you know what's in your 'transferable toolkit'. This toolkit will be your secret weapon to help you make the jump to a different industry, move departments in your current company or perhaps go freelance. Whatever move you want to make, having the right toolkit will make it more effortless and achievable.

SECTION 3:

REMIND YOURSELF THAT YOU ARE AWESOME

CHAPTER 5

EVALUATE YOUR TOOLKIT

Most of the people I work with have no idea what their skills, work passions or strengths are and how they may be underusing certain strengths. Whenever I ask the people I coach to name their strengths, I usually get a lot of blank stares and mumbles. This applies to us all. But ask us to list our weaknesses and we can't wait to share.

'Ooh so I hate…'

'I don't think I'm very good at…'

'I can't/don't know how to…'

Why is it so difficult for us to nail down what we love and excel at? In this chapter, I want to help you do exactly this. You are in for a treat.

Together we will explore how knowing and understanding your strengths and skills can help you get to the bottom of why you are unhappy at work. Walking through your career journey to date helps to unpick the skills that can best serve you, especially if you want to move into a different industry/job/role or want to pitch yourself for opportunities and projects (some of which might not exist yet). Equally, identifying your passions and values can help you pinpoint where something feels a bit sour in your current work and what you aspire to find elsewhere perhaps.

What's in your toolkit?

Strengths, skills, passions and values. What's the real difference?

Strengths – an area you are naturally good at and didn't have to learn. Those that come easy to me are problem-solving, listening, empathizing and remaining calm. What about you? Are you naturally curious or patient or methodical? Knowing your strengths will help you demonstrate that you are 'the best type of person' for a job or task.
Skills – something you can learn and acquire through repetition, either on the job or through study. For instance, learning Japanese (I'm still trying to master this myself), programming code, designing and delivering art-therapy sessions or, in my case, coaching people to find work they love. These are the elements you can match to the ones a future employer is looking for in an industry or sector you want to work in. You can offer direct value to a company or organization by distinguishing and matching your skills to a role/task.
Passions – I have a deep motivation to help people strive to be their best and find work they love. It gets me out of bed, even when I'm feeling sick. What's your passion? What are you most enthusiastic about?
Values – let's just call this a personal code or judgement of what is important in your life. These are standards that you hold yourself to and what you want others to see in you too.

I'm going to talk you through each of these, giving you action steps I want you to take as well as exercises to bring it to life.

Strengths

When we apply our strengths:

- the day flies by
- we have more confidence and less stress
- we are more engaged, creative and satisfied with our work

Here are the 20 core strengths that I've identified in my time working with a range of clients:

1. Polymath Learning is so sexy to you! Waxing lyrical on new subjects, random pieces of knowledge and facts fills you with glee.	**2. Narrator** Let me take you on a journey! Always one to craft an epic story out of the mundane to surprise and delight any audience.
3. Fire-starter Anyone need a lighter? You've got the power to ignite new creativity or inject innovation into tired situations or ways of thinking.	**4. Balancer** You like helping people to reach a compromise for the greater good. Peace is what you seek and you strive to help create that in times of tension and discord.
5. Tactical You are logical and strategic. You love to cut through the crap to get to a decision and provide everyone with a roadmap.	**6. Brainiac** As a deep thinker, you like to reflect on great ideas and solutions before making decisions.
7. Rapport builder You love nothing better than appreciating and understanding how others feel and doing what you can to make sure they always feel positive.	**8. Acrobat** Whatever the situation you can adapt, shapeshift, balance or mould yourself to it. You hate being boxed in.
9. Leader You always put your hand up first, ready to highlight the best way forward. You can always rally people towards a common goal.	**10. Evaluator** Facts, data and numbers give you the confidence to make clear and effective decisions. You have a strong analytical mind.
11. Conqueror You are a natural competitor and driven by a determination to excel. Success is more than just coming in first to you, it's about making sure you employ your skills to the best use possible.	**12. Fixer** Fixing problems makes your heart sing! You don't shy away from a messy situation or issue that needs solving.
13. Mentor Potential is like a hidden gem that you like to unearth in other people. Through asking questions and being curious, you will coax and tease out people's hidden talents to help them excel.	**14. Virtuous** You are upstanding with high moral standards that you won't compromise for anyone. Working in scenarios that compromise your values feels like a drag.
15. Creator Always brimming with radical suggestions, new objectives, recommendations and goals.	**16. Solo warrior** I don't need any help! That's often your first and last thought. You prefer to satisfy your needs without outside interference.

17. Hopeful Always looking on the bright side and seeing optimism at every angle.	**18. Committed** You love to keep your promises! You believe actions matter most and hate to disappoint others without good reason. If you say you'll do something, you will never be flimsy with your word.
19. Methodical Did someone say spreadsheet, to-do lists and project plans? These are your guilty pleasures that help you achieve your goals.	**20. Considered** One foot in front of the other for you. No point rushing yourself, you enjoy taking your time, cogitating over one problem at a time. Your plans are well thought through.

You may be thinking: OK, sounds great, but how do I find out which ones are MY strengths? Luckily for you I have a Strengths Test available (see page 239). I'm spoiling you I know! Go and take a look, but hurry back to see how it all comes together for you.

EXERCISE

Show me my superpowers

Sometimes our strengths make us feel superhuman and there are other times when charging forward with a particular strength alone can be like a bull rampaging in a china shop.

With everything in life, it's about finding the right balance. This is when you have to think about the spectrum of where your strengths best serve you according to each situation. Most of the time, if you look back at past performance reviews where particular problems or issues were highlighted, they probably related to overused strengths.

Take, for example, my client Serena. Her top 5 strength scores came back as the following:

- Virtuous – she always needs to align her actions to her set principles and ways of doing things
- Tactical – able to see the bigger picture quicker than others and knows the best way to reach the end goal in a heartbeat
- Conqueror – competition is the name of the game for her! After all, what's the point of participating in any challenge if she isn't playing to win?
- Methodical – she loves working to a plan with pace and hates ambiguity
- Fixer – she loves to scrutinize a problem to find a solution, often persisting when other people have long given up

But repeatedly she found it difficult to work well in certain situations and grew frustrated when her ideas weren't taken on board when all she wanted to do was fix the problem.

Weaknesses mainly occur because of two core areas:

Weak spots: Where we hold ourselves back because of a strength we don't have or do very well. Serena's inability to mentor and coach her direct reports was something she was acutely aware of. Instead of avoiding this, she asked her colleague if she could shadow her in the next set of performance review sessions to provide her with some feedback on what she could do better.

Overuse of core strengths: Serena's attitude of 'I've got all the answers' consistently frustrated her co-workers. Her very fixed views meant she was quick to diminish what others had to say and she refused to explore other points of view on the table. When we consistently lean into one strength all the time it can make others feel devalued and anxious. When Serena relaxed a little and asked herself 'What might the shoe be like on the other foot?', inviting her co-workers to propose other ways of thinking and creating, she was able to exercise more patience and understanding. With a lot of practice, she got there!

I don't want you to get into a funk here thinking about your weaknesses or focusing heavily on what's gone wrong in the past. Our brains are wired to look for negativity as a fact of survival. This doesn't mean that you should ignore your weaknesses, but it does mean that you should be realistic about the effort and commitment it takes to form new strengths. A good solution is to mitigate your weaknesses through some constructive self-reflection time (for example, journalling at the end of the day about what went well and what didn't) and working with someone who can help you plug your own gaps with their complementary strengths.

Skills

Employers are essentially looking for evidence that you have the skills to make a difference, otherwise it's a waste of time for both of you and nobody's got time for that. What are the skills needed for most jobs? Where do you excel? Where are you a bit rusty?

Below is a list of some of the key skills I have identified in my work with a wide range of companies. Of course, when it comes to software programs these can vary depending on the type of industry you work in and your role, so the examples below are really designed to prompt you to consider what is, or what might become, a key software program in your chosen industry.

Human relations: social and emotional intelligence

- Coaching
- Advocating
- Social skills
- Persuading
- Active listening

Design and conceptualizing: generating ideas, creating future products or identifying ways to overcome a particular challenge

- Anticipating problems
- Coming up with new ideas
- Identifying the pain points
- Defining the problems

Communication: exchanging, distilling and transmitting ideas

- Storytelling
- Writing copy
- Making presentations
- Facilitating discussions
- Negotiating

Organization and management: directing, guiding, leading people/ teams to bring plans to life

- Mediating
- Supervising
- Setting tasks and priorities
- Teaching
- Motivating

Research and planning: seeking out the knowledge, data and clues to bring products or services to life

- Analysing data
- Formulating a hypothesis
- Critical thinking
- Investigating
- Distinguishing between good and useless information

Familiarity with computer programs/software: from using basic office software all the way to computer programming

- Creating 3D designs
- Building websites
- Editing documents in cloud-based software
- Managing spreadsheets

How do you rate your skills?

As you peruse the list, you may have seen a skill that you smiled at, thinking 'Ooh I love doing that!'. There may have been a few that made you think 'Arghh, I suck at that'. It's worthwhile taking a step back and analysing your current job and maybe two other potential jobs that interest you to see which skills crossover and where you might need to pick up a few more skills.

EXERCISE

The skills gap

Let's have a look at the example below from a former client called Sebastian. Sebastian had been working as a nurse in an Intensive Care Unit but was ready to make a change and move into the field of event design and planning. Since planning his own wedding, he had fallen in love with the process and knew it was something he wanted to do for all types of events.

Together we looked at where we would need to extend his skills range and where the gaps were. In the table that follows, I've highlighted the most pertinent skills we looked at.

SKILLS	JOB ROLES	
	Senior nurse	**Event planner**
Human relations Coaching Advocating Social skills Persuading Active listening	COACHING Works well to mentor and guide junior nurses. ADVOCATING Always advocating for the best for his patients and his team. SOCIAL SKILLS / ACTIVE LISTENING Amazing bedside manner, great listener and can build rapport with all types of people.	COACHING Probably not much need to coach his clients and he won't have a team to start with. SOCIAL SKILLS / ACTIVE LISTENING He will still need to be a great listener, dealing with client requests and navigating conversations with different suppliers. PERSUADING He may need to develop his ability to persuade to ensure his clients buy into the ideas he has up his sleeve.

SKILLS	JOB ROLES	
	Senior nurse	**Event planner**
Design and conceptualizing Anticipating problems. Coming up with new ideas. Identifying the pain points. Defining the problems.	ANTICIPATING and DEFINING PROBLEMS The ICU is a melting pot of problems and emergencies which require quick thinking and solutions. Sebastian has honed this skill massively. NEW IDEAS Not much opportunity to do this as any new ideas for staff or the work environment are often shut down or buried under layers of red tape. He is tired of making suggestions that never come to fruition.	ANTICIPATING and DEFINING PROBLEMS Working as an event planner definitely will call on Sebastian's ability to anticipate problems and pain points, as well as quickly fix things, especially on event day. NEW IDEAS Sebastian will have to delve deeper into his ability to create ideas for his clients. The opportunity to be creative in his current job is limited so he stopped dreaming. The solutions always ended up being staid or predictable.
Communication Storytelling. Writing copy. Making presentations. Facilitating discussion. Negotiating.	FACILITATING DISCUSSIONS Communication, as part of Sebastian's job, has been about facilitating discussions between senior management and his team. MAKING PRESENTATIONS Not one for big presentations or storytelling. He hates public speaking; his communication abilities have always been about relaying facts, status reports, patient treatment plans and rotas.	STORYTELLING Stepping into this career change will call on Sebastian to learn how to take clients on a journey so that they can visualize their perfect event. MAKING PRESENTATIONS Presentations, mood boards and the ability to communicate with visuals over words will be key for Sebastian.

SKILLS	JOB ROLES	
	Senior nurse	**Event planner**
Organization and management Mediating. Supervising. Setting tasks and priorities. Teaching. Motivating.	SETTING PRIORITIES This is his forte in his current role. He loves organizing and running a tight ship of nurses. MEDIATING When tempers fray in his team, Sebastian's level-headedness means that he's able to keep the peace.	SETTING PRIORITIES This is where Sebastian would have the greatest skill transference as organization was his highest strength. He loved setting priorities and following through with action and knows this would serve him well on big event projects. MEDIATING For his clients, Sebastian will have to use his mediating skills to make sure their needs are met and while he navigates the demands of his suppliers.
Research and planning Analysing data. Formulating a hypothesis. Critical thinking. Investigating. Distinguishing between good and useless information.	ANALYSING DATA Sebastian was astute at analysing patient data to make quick decisions or help his team find better answers to critical cases.	ANALYSING DATA He will need to research new suppliers and analyse tender offers from suppliers as well as formulating the best practical routes and options for his client, depending on their budgets.
Familiarity with computer programs/ software Creating 3D designs. Building websites. Editing documents in cloud-based software. Managing spreadsheets	BASIC COMPUTER SKILLS Sebastian is familiar with mail and office programs.	NO SPECIALISED COMPUTER PROGRAM USE He was keen to learn the software related to this industry and decided to seek key courses.

Now that I've given you a head start, maybe you have a few potential career shifts in mind – if you don't, perhaps revisit Chapter 4 and look at what came up in your B.R.I.D.G.E. exercise. But be honest with yourself about how some of your skills may be malleable and which ones you will have to learn. Knowing how to articulate this will help when we come to Chapter 9 and address job changes and interviews.

Passions

Don't worry. I'm not about to launch into a 'forget all this and just follow your passions' speech, but while skills and strengths are necessary to feeling that you are doing a job 'well' and being somewhat satisfied with it, the magic ingredient is the addition of purpose, passion and meaning.

You might be wondering at this point, '*How do I find my passions?*' Well, let's take a trip down memory lane. I want you to think of the activities you enjoyed as a child.

When I was little, I loved making my dad a small, pretend parcel of goodness from leftover dough that my mum would use to make dumplings for her signature chicken soup. He'd arrive home from work looking tired and in need of a pick-me-up. Using the dough, I would form a little basket and then fill it with bits of chocolate or fruit, which I'd then bake. I wasn't exactly Nigella Lawson, but I loved the idea of making him something and I'd serve it on a pretty plate. He'd pretend to love it too while he told me about the ups and downs of his day. Needless to say, this mirrors my current life: experimenting with recipes (I'm much better now) and feeding my friends, actively listening to others, being curious about them and noticing the non-verbal cues people give off.

EXERCISE

Passion party

Step 1

Think of three activities you enjoyed when you were younger. For example:

- Painting nature
- Making and selling cakes
- Watching sci-fi films and reading comics
- Playing with a toy doctor's medical kit
- Building tents in the living room with old sheets

Step 2

Now I want you to think about how particular elements of this activity might be missing in your current job and life. How would it contribute more to your work happiness if you revisited it? Here are some client examples:

- Playing with your doctor's medical kit: *'I gave up on pursuing a career in medicine, I wish I hadn't. I'm really passionate about alternative therapies. Why am I not working in this area right now?'*

- Building tents in the living room with old sheets: *'Currently I work as an economics lecturer, but I want to write and tell stories. I enjoy creating worlds of fantasy and play, and being able to transport others to different dimensions. I wonder how I can inject more of this storytelling into my lectures instead of sticking to this tired format. My students might have more fun too with this difficult subject!'*

- Making and selling cakes: *'My parents were strict with pocket money. I had to come up with creative ways to get pocket money to buy all the comics. Being a good baker, I started to create ingenious and radical flavour combinations to sell. How the hell did I end up settling for a salary and a job I hate now? I need to go freelance. I'm great at reading the market and coming up with unique products and offerings. I miss that challenge, the creative freedom to play and earn more money.'*

Step 3

Can you see any link to your passions in the answers you gave to the following questions from the exercise 'Career Daydreams' (see page 26)?

- *If all jobs paid your dream monthly income, what would you really like to do? (What ideas have you been holding back on due to money concerns?)*
- *If you could speak to your 16-year-old self and offer some work-happiness advice, what would you say?*

Which passion is trying to shine through but feels stifled, and why?

Most of the time, this exercise gives us a steer on our deepest passions, motivations and desires. It's also a look into what passions we may have left behind as we got busy with life and adulting. Perhaps there is something you want to reintroduce into your life and your work.

Don't be alarmed if you turned an old passion into your profession and now feel like you've exhausted it. This happens and, in most cases, the next step is to explore what other areas around this particular passion could excite you. Or it might be that using that passion as a hobby is enough.

I want to introduce you to a client of mine called Emmanuel and how he revived his love for his passion that had turned into a career trough.

Emmanuel loved drawing and creating graphic designs and other visual stories. After studying art and design at university he found his way into a role as an art director. However, the buzz of working in the field was slowly wearing thin. The commercial work was no longer captivating him and he wanted to work more with his hands as well as explore the world of photography. The higher up Emmanuel became in his field, he realized he was just managing others instead of hands-on creating. Attending some life drawing and photography classes started to revive his earlier childhood passions for building and designing things from scratch. Soon, he started attending more classes and was invited to contribute to an exhibition. Then he began to mentor budding artists one day a week, after negotiating Fridays off from work to do this. Mentoring people from different ages and backgrounds gave him a renewed vision and appetite for the creative industry and photography. Emmanuel came alive helping them bring all their imaginative approaches to life, and found pleasure in connecting them with people, opportunities and the odd paid project within his company. Work took on a whole new meaning.

Values

What are things you won't compromise on? Honesty? Trustworthiness? Originality? Values are the principles that are personal to you, that you live and die by. You can sometimes become worn down when you feel your values are compromised by situations or people.

EXERCISE

The values quiz

When you work in a company or with people that misalign with your values, you know something feels off but it can be hard to pinpoint what exactly is squashing your work happiness. This little exercise will help you decipher your core values, how to communicate them and seek work that doesn't jar with them. Rate the statements listed below using the following points:

Hell no... that's not me = 1 point
Hmm, a little bit true = 2 points
Getting closer to the truth = 3 points
Spot on, that's so true! = 4 points

Think about your gut instinct. What feels right for you, your work-happiness aspirations and personal life? If you are a bit hesitant because you feel strong personally about one value but rank it lower on the scale for your work happiness, I would urge you to base your choice on your work happiness first over personal. After all, we are doing this to help you find work environments and colleagues you want to gravitate towards.

OK, let's get started:

1. I want to understand the 'nitty gritty' of those that I work with and hold close.

2. I love reinventing something and looking at ways to do things differently.

3. I like people to know that they can turn to me if they need someone strong to lean on.

4. I enjoy being a risk taker; life is too short.

5. I think what I bring to the table leaves a lasting impression on people.

6. I love to share my true desires and thoughts with those around me and be honest about my life.

7. I have natural leadership qualities.

8. People often admire and praise the way I am.

9. I believe I am a strong character.

10. I need work, things and people with substance in my life... It's not all about style without substance.

11. I try to live my life free from constraints.

12. I like to make sure I have all the facts before I make a decision.

13. I hate feeling that I am stagnating, I love change.

14. I hate ambiguity or inconsistency in a person's actions and words.

15. I think about what footprint I leave behind for others. I want to know that what I do will benefit others.

16. I make choices that are eclectic and different from the norm.

17. There is always room for further development or to build on existing ideas.

18. I'd rather have a few cherished friends/co-workers than lots.

19. I adore history. I love to look back and see the origins of something, look at how things are made and what learnings we can use to move forward.

20. I tell it like it is... I am what I am...

21. I pride myself on being exceptional at whatever I decide to master.

The results are in!

Below are seven 'Love It or Leave It' values (this is by no means an exhaustive list but gives you a chance to generate more).

I want you to add up the values you have for each statement. The higher totals show your predominant values and the lower scores indicate your less-important values. If you have the same number for two or more of the values, just pick the TOP FOUR from the group.

Add statements 1, 10, 18.
Your **Connection** score is...

Add statements 2, 13, 17.
Your **Newness** score is...

Add statements 4, 11, 16.
Your **Spirited** score is...

Add statements 5, 15, 19.
Your **Timeless** score is...

Add statements 6, 14, 20.
Your **Truth** score is...
Add statements 8, 12, 21.
Your **Proficiency** score is...

Add statements 3, 7, 9.
Your **Strength** score is...

What are your top four 'Love It or Leave It' values?

What does a high Connection score mean for you?

You are a lovely soul who really values getting to know people. You love to support and empathize with co-workers, customers and clients, showing them that you care and really value them. You make people feel alive and welcomed. Your personal brand is one of adding value wherever you can and being a reliable person for others to seek understanding.

Other words for Connection: contribution, love, altruism.

How to seek work that meets your value: It's important to seek work that gives you the opportunity to contribute and work with others, a team or someone on a deep level. It can be hard if you become a freelancer and have not built a community around you to support working solo, so make this a priority if this is one of your values. Your work needs to offer the ability for you to make a difference to others or a larger cause.

What does a high value of Newness show?

You are an individual striving for revolution, modernization and a good ol' shake up. You love rousing others to transform, change and move beyond obstacles. You want to be used as an instrument to help people dream and push the boundaries of imagination. Your personal brand is all about change, creativity, development and progression.

Other words for Newness: innovation, artistry, expression.

How to seek work that meets your value: You are the flag-bearer for change and therefore you love being in work environments that provide you with opportunities to meet new people, work on different projects simultaneously or travel. Could working for yourself give you the ability to do something different every other day? Or perhaps a shift in departments could provide the landscape for you to share more of your cutting-edge opinions and allow you to set the agenda. Does your current role offer you the ability to flourish?

Love high energy and vibrancy in your life? If Spirited is a high value for you, it shows up like this:

You are self-assured, energetic and dynamic. Your *joie de vivre* motivates people. You are bold and living your life your way in technicolour.

Other words for Spirited: playful, enthusiastic.

How to seek work that meets your value: You hate being told what to do and feeling like you have to dim your light. It's worth thinking about which office environments either elevate or dampen your mood. It might be that working in an office isn't your bag and perhaps you want to be outdoors, working in nature or with kids. Or maybe you fancy a co-working space surrounded by lots of start-up and entrepreneurial energy.

Love all things heritage and traditional? Is Timeless one of your values?

You really value leaving your imprint or mark for a long time to come and you want to help others carve out their place in history too. You build long-lasting relationships and value longevity. You are thoughtful, compassionate and selective about how you spend your time and money.

Other words for Timeless: depth, heritage, tradition.

How to seek work that meets your value: You value companies that have a purpose and a vision with depth. Perhaps you want to help brands with better ways to build long-term relationships with their customers. Or maybe you want to work in a boutique company that has a small, trusted pool of clients, preferring quality over quantity instead of a monolithic company with lots of brands and products.

Always keen to get to the heart of the matter? If Truth is a top scoring value for you, it looks like this:

You value being upfront and honest. People know what to expect from you. You love helping others find a clear path through obstacles as they can trust that you walk the talk.

Other words for Truth: clarity, simplicity, purity.

How to seek work that meets your value: You seek consistency in your work and surroundings. Ambiguity and indifference drive you mad and you can sniff out when something isn't quite right. You want to work on projects that matter, and have an end goal that is transparent.

Like precision and accuracy? If so, Proficiency is a value for you

You have high standards and expectations, and everything is turned up a notch when people are in your presence. You value seeing how it all fits together and creating the optimum solution with your expert analysis. People warm to you because you are measured and pay attention to the fine print.

Other words for Proficiency: accuracy, polished, excellence.

How to seek work that meets your value: When people come to you, they have made the decision to settle for nothing less than excellence and that's what you expect from your work environment too. You like sharp decision-making and high-pressured stakes that require quick smarts.

Are you bold, confident and resilient? Strength is your value!

What a determined individual you are! You are driven by your resolute thinking to implement change and take the lead. People naturally see you as a force to be reckoned with and you feel happy to slot into that position. Some of your magic is bound to rub off on your colleagues as they look to you for direction.

Other words for Strength*:* resolute, bold, influential.

How to seek work that meets your value: You want to have the power to make tough decisions, call the shots and shape the course of future activities and agendas. You can weather any storm and may value working in conditions that require you to take risks, create change in a newly merged company or lead large teams, some of whom are a distance away.

Connecting the dots

How does this all connect? After spending many evenings working through my career options, I was able to find routes that I wanted to take and ones I wanted to leave behind.

It's time to bring all this intel together for you too. I want you to think of your last three roles and write out the following:

- Role – title or what were you working on
- Tasks and responsibilities – day-to-day activities
- Strengths used – the core strengths you used or had the opportunity to use
- Weak spots – which areas did you struggle with or need help with?
- Skills – what skills did you use from the list above?
- Passions – how did this work align to a particular passion, if at all?
- Values – did this work fit in or clash with your values?

By comparing three of your past roles, you can start to tease out and identify what types of roles do not play consistently to your strengths, skills, passions or values. I know it can be frustrating as hell when you work in a job that doesn't feel like the right fit. The days drag on and you end up doubting your abilities and losing your confidence. In the next two exercises, I want you to get super clear and join up all the dots to give you some powerful statements for your next steps forward.

EXERCISE

Connecting the dots – Part 1

Here's one example from my own life.

ROLE or TITLE	Account manager for an advertising agency
TASKS	Client liaison and management. Research and product development. Helping to deliver projects by communicating with creative and production teams.
STRENGTHS USED (Refer to the Strengths in this chapter, see pages 60–4)	• Tactical – big visionary, able to see the bigger goal. • Fixer – able to distil a problem and find the best way to deal with a difficult situation.
SKILLS (Refer to the Skills in this chapter, see pages 65–9)	Strong emphasis on skills such as: • Organization and management – making sure creative and production teams met deadlines and delivered campaigns on time for my client. • Communication – delivering pitches and presentations. • Research and planning – finding consumer data on the behaviour of young women and children. • Designing and conceptualizing – designing ingenious ways to market new cereal products.
INDUSTRY	Advertising and branding
PASSIONS (Refer to the Passions in this chapter, see pages 70–3)	Didn't really play to my passion for supporting others, seeing the development of others. Products and services I worked on served a wide 'faceless' audience with no one-to-one work.
VALUES (Refer to the Values in this chapter, see pages 73–9)	My core values are Connection and Spirited. I have to feel connected to a wider and deeper goal and unfortunately the products I worked on just didn't engage me.

As I progressed through my career roles and journeys, patterns formed around the work I kept gravitating towards. I wanted:

- To use my creative problem-solving skills and strengths to focus more on issues to do with people instead of products and services
- To coach and mentor people instead of just working behind a screen, collating data on website impressions and sales figures
- The feeling that I was helping to make change a reality

EXERCISE

Connecting the dots – Part 2

I'd like you to complete the following using Sebastian's case as a guide. When it's your turn, fill in your own answers in place of the examples in italics.

- I want a career that builds on and transfers my signature strengths AND skills which are around... [*organizing and troubleshooting*]

  ....

  ....

- Deep down, I'm someone who is passionate about... [*people and making them feel good and happy. I just don't think nursing is the place that I'm best served to do this.*]

  ....

  ....

- I want to grow in new ways by... [*building on my communications skills to tell stories both verbally and visually, learn how to influence decisions and generate better ideas that aren't so rigid, logical and formulaic*]

  ....

  ....

- The industries or subjects which keep me engaged are... [*fashion, interiors, event planning and styling*]

  ....

  ....

Phew, you've got your toolkit!

Identifying your strengths, skills and passions was never going to be a quick task. But you did it! Well done.

Analysing yourself can feel really uncomfortable, but now you know just how awesome you are. Grab yourself a little treat. You deserve it!

Did any of the following thoughts surface for you, perhaps?

- I know my passions, but why do I never follow my gut?
- Damn, I keep playing small and not going for what really excites me. I struggle with change.
- The majority of my current strengths and skills *are applicable elsewhere*. I only need to push myself to use them in different ways. What the hell is stopping me?
- Am I even ready to make these changes? I've been talking about this for years.

It's one thing to talk about skills and potential ways we'd like to fulfil our passions but taking the next step can seem hard.

Don't worry I'm not going to leave you out at sea without a float! In the next chapter, we are going to zap those inklings of doubt, bolster your ability to set some goals and get you dancing with risk and experimenting with your new ideas before you commit. Come on. What are you waiting for?

CHAPTER 6

MAKING FRIENDS WITH CHANGE

You might have picked up this book intent on one route, but perhaps you've now made a U-turn. That's all part of the process. Remember the winding road I told you about?

In this chapter, I want to help you overcome decision fatigue and identify ways to build your yellow brick road. If you don't visualize some realistic goals and process how you navigate change, you can end up stagnating and in analysis-paralysis land. Sharpening your decision-making skills will enable you to make peace with your decisions and move forward, free of your burdens.

Priming yourself for change

Change doesn't happen overnight. It's a process of many invisible forces that can either speed up or slow down.

Think about how long you take to make changes in your life. Are you an early adopter, leaning into the headwind and seizing every opportunity to embrace the new? Do you limp wearily into changes with trepidation or fear, or do you have to be dragged, kicking and screaming, to make necessary changes?

I've worked with individuals of all ages and I've noticed a trend in the waves of emotion, anxiety, awareness and effort they exhibit as they respond to tensions and concerns around changes at work. Take a look at them here:

Phase	In plain English...	It shows up as...
1. Oblivious	You are ignorant to the idea that you need change and to where you are really suffering. Lots of hints from others suggesting you make changes.	• Unwillingness to get help • Suppressing the pain or making excuses • Lack of awareness of other indicating factors like stress, illness, decreased mental or physical wellbeing • Statements like 'I'm fine', 'It's nothing', 'I'm OK'
2. The 'aha' moment'	Suddenly the penny drops. I have a problem! However, you are running both towards and away from the changes you may need to make.	• Rationalizing • Debating the obstacles • Second-guessing yourself: 'I'm too old to change jobs', 'I can't afford to quit', 'My manager won't like my proposal', 'I tried new hobbies before. It didn't work'
3. Admission	If I don't do something about this now, I'm an idiot!	• Realizing the damage that staying in a job you are ambivalent about causes to you, your health and mind as well as to others around you • Allowing yourself to say the words 'I need help' • Buying this book • Weighing up your options
4. Movement	Less talk and more action.	• Creating a plan • Mapping out some goals and strategies • Reaching out for support • Seeking professional help • Being mindful of your excuses and where you are likely to backtrack
5. Picking up speed	Keeping your happiness levels topped up for the journey	• Putting processes and strategies in place to prevent you changing your mind or doing a U-turn • Tackling your mindset so that you stay on the path to success
6. Backtrack	When you slip into old habits.	• Getting stuck and veering off course • Analysis paralysis – meaning you revert back to the safety of the 'known' over making a decision • Discontent with progress and quitting too soon • Going back to square one

Do you recognize yourself in any of these phases? Have you progressed through a few stages, are you right at the beginning or have you regressed?

Getting stuck is part of the journey. If it was all a piece of cake, people would be switching roles and shifting careers in a heartbeat. But this topic will forever be a sticky subject unless we embrace the rollercoaster. Birth and destruction are always brought about by pain, anguish and intensity. The best way to outwit this is by being clear on your hopes, goals and your capability to pick the right path for you.

Taking the elevator to your best outcome!

I want you to imagine yourself about to step into an elevator that will take you to your wildest career dreams at the penthouse floor. But in order to discover them, you need to take a moment and first discuss what each floor has to show you about what you've achieved, what you want to learn more about and what you want to create for yourself.

Here, I want to look at how we can visualize different situations instead of milling over what's not working.

Floor one – this floor is a celebration of all the top wins in your career, when you have felt very much aligned to your work, when you felt inspired and when you performed at your peak.

Floor five – this floor allows you to look at what dreams and desires you hold for your future work happiness. These are some of the biggest aspirations that you hold dear to your heart and that you would like to make a reality.

Floor ten – this is the floor that provides clarity on all the tools you will need to use, the people to connect with, the skills you might need to learn and the available opportunities to help bring your dream from floor five to fruition. Everything you need to succeed is available on this floor.

Floor fifteen – this floor is where you can imagine taking your first baby step on the ladder (see the next section on goals). What is that first rung? Can you achieve it this week? This month?

Penthouse – this is the floor where you reach your ultimate dream of work happiness. What are you doing? Who are you surrounded by?

Here is the journey taken by one of my clients, Tanya:

Floor one

Tanya was at a pivotal point between staying in or leaving her job as Environment Manager for a small charity. On floor one, she realized that she had pulled off some amazing projects with a great team by her side. By going through some of the exercises we explored in Chapter 4, she outlined all the positive aspects of her job, which helped her realize that she had the power and opportunity to mould it into something even better. These realizations trumped leaving and branching out on her own as a consultant.

Floor five

A big dream for Tanya was to learn a few more time-management skills as a leader, which would give her more opportunities in her working week for her own professional development and also allow her to take better control of her Mondays off, which had become blurred with work. As a manager, she struggled to carve out her own learning needs and stay on top of industry changes. She wanted to be a great resource for her team but felt like she wasn't abreast of innovations and inspiration.

Floor ten

Tanya's visualization here was made up of four pathways:

1. Pinpoint the leadership traits she admired in her colleagues and approach them with a proposal to skill-share so that she could gain some 'unofficial' mentoring or advice from them while also offering reciprocal help.
2. Better planning and delegation so that her team wasn't always racing to meet deadlines and she didn't have to spend her Mondays off catching up or dealing with work overflow.
3. Map out key professional conferences she wanted to attend, contribute to and potentially speak at.
4. Potentially talk with her boss about facilitating a session around better workflow communication and time management at the next Senior Leadership Strategy retreat.

Floor fifteen

Tanya imagined that her first practical step was to re-establish boundaries with her team and get everyone on the same page with weekly check-ins and workflow. This step would help her to empower them to make better decisions so that she didn't need to constantly firefight.

Penthouse

A smoother working week, with Mondays clear to explore personal and professional interests; stronger self-leadership to plan her weeks better, and more open and honest communication with her team.

The way we talk about ourselves and our futures is a powerful means of creating new realities. These new images and visualizations prompt new actions and behaviours. What you choose to focus on becomes your reality and this process allows you to bring the best of the past into creating a confident future.

EXERCISE

The dream elevator

Close your eyes and imagine yourself walking into a lift. Press the button for floor one, up you go and listen for the ping. The door opens – what do you see?

Floor one:

....

....

Floor five:

....

....

Floor ten:

....

....

Floor fifteen:

....

....

Penthouse:

....

....

Getting S.M.A.R.T.

Now we have created the vision, it's time to set out the goals. How do you currently set goals? Or are you just twisting in the wind? You've probably heard of S.M.A.R.T. goals, but your attitude to how you set your goals will in turn set the tone for successful work happiness. Whether your goals are to aim for the bravest thing you've ever tried in your working life or to break through a glass ceiling in your industry, set them out following my examples below:

Specific

Avoid ambiguous and unclear: *I want to update my CV.*

Be targeted and practical: *I'll create several versions of my CVs ready to send out by Monday morning*

Measurable

Avoid ambiguous and unclear: *I'll contact my references.*

Be targeted and practical: *I will identify one reference for each of my past work experiences, send them my updated CV and ask them for the help within one month*

Attainable

Avoid ambiguous and unclear: *Learn new 3D-modelling software by next week.*

Be targeted and practical: *Create 30 rendered drawings for my portfolio*

Relevant

Avoid ambiguous and unclear: *I want to volunteer.*

Be targeted and practical: *I'd like to set up a workplace mentoring scheme as I'm keen to help younger employees progress into the right senior positions.*

Time bound

Avoid ambiguous and unclear: *I want to learn Spanish outside of work.*

Be targeted and practical: *I want to be able to navigate Valencia by my holiday in April*

A ladder metaphor will help you realize your S.M.A.R.T. goals and bring them to life. Plus, it is quite aspirational seeing it as a ladder and elevating yourself with each step up, so now try the next exercise.

EXERCISE

The ladder

Think about a big goal you'd like to achieve in the next 6–12 months and draw a ladder:

Top of the ladder – the primary goal you aspire to right now.

- ➤ To fall in love with your job and earn more money
- ➤ To leave your job and start a business

Rungs to the top = long-term goals – monthly targets over 6–12 months are 6–12 rungs on your ladder and are the stepping stones required to get to the top rung or goal. What do you need to do each month to get to the prize?

- ➤ Work towards your monthly actions to make sure you get your pay increase within the next 6–9 months
- ➤ Investigate several business ideas before choosing one route

Habit-forming recurring goals – these are spaces between the rungs and short-term actions needed to reach your long-term goals. This is what do you need to do daily/weekly/monthly, regardless of what else is going on.

- ➤ Prepare your research, know your numbers, seek out opportunities for learning. Monitor your performance and your progress
- ➤ Find potential collaborators or partners for your new business idea. Read key magazines and books, check trends, attend networking events related to what you want to move into

It's easy to think that following the ladder is a straight route to success. But it's important to be aware of distractions and conflicting goals, for example, you may want to go for a higher promotion at work even though it conflicts with your desire to be home early and on time every evening. Take the time to identify the gaps, the time spans between achievements and where you might need to get assistance.

Continued overleaf

Next, take a notebook and reflect on the following four questions:

What success/challenges do you face when goal setting?

Factors that impair goal setting include:

- Lack of confidence
- Impatience
- Desire to please
- Overexcitement
- Too much choice

Where are you not setting big enough goals? What are the fears holding you back?

- I will be ridiculed
- I will disappoint X
- I can't make money from that
- I don't have the skills

When you are 'stuck', what will jolt you back into action?

- My support system
- Sticking to my deadlines

What does success look like to you?

It's important that you aren't just setting goals blindly. What values are your goals aligned to and what will be the guiding force that makes you want to achieve them? *Why* do you want to set/achieve these particular goals? Write your answers here:

....

....

....

....

As you progress through this book, I ask you to keep in mind your overarching ideas around success and what goals you would like to reach in whatever path you choose.

Finding the diamond (ideas) in the rough

By now, you should have some goals sorted, right?

Hmm, I can sense a slight hesitation. I expected this. On the one hand, some of you reading this might be raring to go with your new plans. Or maybe you are gearing up to have a conversation with your co-worker about building a better work relationship.

But there may be a few of you thinking, 'I can't set any goals when I still don't quite know which way I want to go or what I really want.' Which one is your killer diamond idea?

Sifting out the gems

What you have to do is tackle some of your ideas, whims, desires and dreams as if they were scientific experiments, sifting out the stones to find the sparkly gems. This means investigating your thought processes, shooting down your assumptions and really getting under the skin of what you keep dreaming about but are not actually doing. Below is a demonstration of how to do this. As you read through each step, have in mind any latent dreams you've been wanting to explore.

1. Make an observation

I'm unhappy at work. That Sunday-night-blues feeling means I just don't want to get to work on Monday.

2. Ask a question

I want to do work I'm passionate about. I have three passions: photography, food and tech. But which one would make me happy?

3. Propose a hypothesis

A *hypothesis* is a potential answer to the question. One that can somehow be tested and experimented with to provide you with some answers.

- Hosting my own supper clubs holds the key to my work happiness.
- I love photography exhibitions. Curating them is my dream job.
- Creating a prototype of my new software idea would be a great way to boost my skill set.

It's a good way to test some of your general ideas and dreams which at the moment feel somewhat amorphous and intangible.

4. Make predictions

A prediction is an outcome we'd expect to see if the hypothesis is correct.

- Prediction: It might be a massive undertaking to run a supper club on my own. I need to explore a few and see how they actually work. Perhaps there's something else I can do that involves food, people and blogging.
- Curating exhibitions is likely to be a lot of fun but I'm not sure how big my repertoire of photography styles needs to be to put on a show that people want to see. I think I'm missing a few steps in the process. What else might I like about photography and exhibitions?
- If I investigate the market, I might find my software idea exists and there might be an easier way to tweak my offering or perhaps collaborate instead of pouring lots of money into it straight away.

5. Test the predictions

Time to experiment. I often say it's worth setting a timeframe to explore your ideas. If you have three ideas, why not spend two months on each so, after six months, you will have a clear idea of your next steps and core goals.

To test the supper-club prediction, make a list of supper clubs to explore over the next two months with key lines of enquiry:

- What inspiration am I looking for when I visit a supper club?
- Do I like crafting menus?
- Could I ask to shadow someone and discover how to bring a supper club to life?
- Which foods or cuisines do I want to focus on?
- Am I keen to explore the connection between food as a way to boost communication among strangers?
- Have I got what it takes, and the time and space to bring one to life?

- Do I like cooking for big groups? Whom might I collaborate with?
- How would I make money?
- I'm interested in reading restaurant reviews. Could I review supper clubs?

Likely outcomes:

- The hypothesis is supported – supper clubs excite you and you enjoy creating experiences for small and large groups. You want to look at how you can use food and eating experiences as a way to help companies create better cultures.
- The hypothesis is not supported. You actually just enjoy eating at supper clubs and it's the discovery of new ideas and meeting new people that you love. In reality, the experiment shows you really want to write or review podcasts about supper clubs, not create and execute your own.

6. Clarify

The last step is to reflect on your results and use them to guide your next steps.

At the end of the six months, which idea would you like to experiment further with? Remember the key to finding happiness at work is to test out your ideas and be open to refining your thoughts each time. The path is a winding one with many twists and turns. In the words of Ralph Waldo Emerson, 'Don't be too timid and squeamish about your actions. All life is an experiment.' Keep this in mind as you read through Chapters 7–10. In Chapter 8, you will get a chance to test out some of your dreams and ideas.

Trusting your three brains

Three? I thought I just had one?

It was research by Paul MacLean, a physician and neuroscientist at Yale University, that first indicated we have three brains, each with 'its own special intelligence, its own subjectivity, its own sense of time and space and its own memory'.

The three brains are known as the neocortex or neo-mammalian brain, the limbic or paleo-mammalian system and the reptilian brain. Each of them operate independently but are connected by nerves to the other two.

We've all heard statements like: 'trust your gut' and 'be true to your heart'. There are in fact three ways we can make a decision, whether it's buying that killer pair of shoes, swiping left or right on a dating app or taking that new job. *We either lead with our head, heart or gut.*

Although the head, heart and gut brains work together, they have very different functions and perform different mental and emotional roles.

The head (neocortex) brain:

- Analyses information and applies logic
- Recognizes patterns
- Provides reasoning to create sense and meaning

An example of this is our endless pros and cons lists.

The heart (limbic) brain:

- Senses the world through emotions and feelings such as anger and joy
- Processes your values, aspirations and connections with those around you

Decisions made by the heart are mostly based around 'I want' instead of 'What I really need is...' They often feel good in the moment but sometimes come with a nasty sinking feeling. For example, impulsive purchases that leave you with buyer's remorse shortly after.

The gut (reptilian) brain:

- Is used for understanding our unique identity and who we are in the world
- Helps us learn self-preservation by teaching us to follow our instinct for protection, boundaries and safety – the 'gut feeling' we experience that at times triggers a fight or flight response

For example, the feeling when you realize that working with a particular client might be a mistake. Your values are not in alignment and, while the money is tempting, you know it might be a disaster and something you will live to regret.

How do we begin to trust that this is the right time for change? Do we go with our head, heart or gut? I say that you need to check in with all three of your brains.

The head, heart and gut have different ways of processing information, people and the world, so you need to learn how to master each of them to help you interrogate your decisions. It's no longer enough to just think logically, you must engage your emotions and deploy a 'gut check'.

If you don't use your head, decisions are not thoroughly analysed or investigated. Without the heart, you will not operate from a place of deep personal value or genuine care for yourself. When you ignore your gut, you won't have the willpower to act, which will result in passively sitting back and letting things happen to you that aren't in your best interest.

On the next page, I've devised an exercise to help you get to grips with how your three brains work.

EXERCISE

The three-brain check-in

I want you to break down some of your ideas or potential decisions and look at how each is represented by the head, heart and gut brains to help you iron out your choices.

	Head	**Heart**	**Gut**
Move from academia into corporate work	I can see how my background in psychology could be used in the workplace in a variety of ways: looking at mental wellbeing, organizational design or people and culture development.	I feel like I can make a real difference in companies that need better mental health awareness practices for their employees to navigate stress and avoid burning out. I want to use my skills to help more people instead of writing research papers.	I don't feel like I belong in academia any more. It feels stilted to me and I'm tired of working with theories. I want to see how it works in real life. It's time to earn more money as I get older with more responsibilities. Plus I want to buy a house, which I can't do on my research salary.

Build your stamina – the signature personality traits of entrepreneurship

So far I've given you guidelines on how to prep for change. As we continue to challenge those change muscles, I want to offer a few last words on how to tackle your work-happiness transitions with an entrepreneurial mindset.

Hmm, you might be thinking, but I don't know if I want to be an entrepreneur.

That's OK. It's more about the attitude you need to have on this journey to stay the course, whichever path you choose. In a changing work landscape, you need to have grit, dexterity and stamina. Drawing on my work with clients and studying business owners I admire, I've created a list of traits, which I believe are a direct correlation to success:

1. Visionary: able to paint a picture of the future and your career desires.
2. Passionate: full of gusto around a desired ambition to reach your work-happiness goals.
3. Not work-shy: willing to do what it takes to succeed, be it early mornings or late nights.
4. Spot the gaps and connect the dots: identify the missing links, bridging the gaps in your skills and making connections between your strengths and the opportunities available.
5. Confident: strong inner belief and slight arrogance (but not too much) to avoid wavering when voices of dissent increase.
6. Adaptable: willing to bob and weave as the tide flows, able to move a few steps back if it means propelling you forward in other areas.
7. Able to sell/market yourself: skilled in the art of persuading others to take a punt on you.
8. Wise with money: comfortable talking about money and managing your finances to avoid anxiety.
9. Not afraid to ask for help and accept help: knowing that nobody is an island on the journey.
10. Able to bounce back repeatedly from adversity: when the sh*t hits the fan, will you cower and hide or say 'I GOT THIS'?

How many of those do you think you have? What do you need to refine them further?

All of these, when executed beautifully, will provide the rich foundations to make your journey a tad bit smoother. I'm not saying it's all smooth sailing, even with most of these qualities, because life is unpredictable, but they will certainly help, whatever path you choose.

Moving from one spot to another

After working through all the exercises, you are now in a rich place of *knowing* about yourself. What's next is for you to move from this primary place of knowledge to the secondary place of *doing and becoming*. Getting to this new, unknown behaviour and exploring all the possibilities can feel like crossing into another realm. Like Narnia or Alice in Wonderland, you may find yourself tempted to question whether you should open that wardrobe door? Dive right in and eat the cake? Do I apply for that job? Do I have that conversation with my boss? You have to be prepared to trial new things, test an idea or step into a challenge. This is about moving from a place of knowing to doing, from one primary behaviour to the secondary behaviour. Take a look at some examples below:

PRIMARY BEHAVIOUR
'I HATE MY BOSS AND I WANT TO LOOK FOR A NEW JOB.'

SECONDARY BEHAVIOUR
WORKING IN A PLACE YOU LOVE WITH A GREAT MANAGER AND COLLEAGUES

PRIMARY BEHAVIOUR
'I'M A SHY PERSON. I'M NOT SURE I CAN SPEAK TO MY BOSS ABOUT A PAY RISE.'

SECONDARY BEHAVIOUR
CLUED-UP EMPLOYEE SUCCESSFULLY SPEAKING TO THEIR BOSS AND EARNING AN EXTRA 10K.

PRIMARY BEHAVIOUR
'I'M A NEWLY SELF-EMPLOYED PERSON, I'VE NEVER HAD TO SELL MYSELF BEFORE.'

SECONDARY BEHAVIOUR
A SAVVY FREELANCER WITH THE PERFECT ELEVATOR PITCH FOR NETWORKING EVENTS.

PRIMARY BEHAVIOUR
'I'VE WORKED IN THE SAME FIELD FOR MOST OF MY CAREER. I DON'T KNOW HOW TO MAKE A SWITCH INTO A DIFFERENT INDUSTRY WITHOUT ANY CONTACTS OR INSIGHTS.'

SECONDARY BEHAVIOUR
AN INDIVIDUAL WITH A BLACK BOOK FULL OF CONNECTORS AND MENTORS READY TO HELP THEM SECURE THEIR NEXT JOB.

As you consider these states, I want to ask you:

- When was the last time you challenged yourself to try something new?
- When was the last time you took a bold step and pushed yourself?

A daredevil step could be having a difficult conversation at work, learning a new skill, mastering your finances or attending a networking event. It's only through appreciating the delicate art of being *comfortable with being uncomfortable* that you can reap great rewards and this secondary state of being. This could be anything from landing that new job you've dreamed about for so long, building your network in a new industry or boosting your confidence and relationships. It's not easy, trust me I know. There were times when I've retreated from challenges but, equally, when I've jolted myself into new actions, I've enjoyed tears of joy, triumph, success and unforeseen wins. What's more important is that you *try* and that you take it at a pace that's right for you.

What type of 'adventurer' will you be?

With all this talk of crossing realms and dancing into new worlds of work happiness, what type of adventurer will you be? How will you cross over to this new behaviour?

Here are three profiles. Have a think about which best describes you:

1. **Cross at the smallest point**

   This is someone who chooses to dip their toes into change. For you, the question is what's the smallest action I can take that's not going to ruffle too many feathers. You like maintaining the status quo while still feeling like some progress is being made.

   Could it be having a conversation with your partner about your desires and your hopes before you take any action?

2. **Progressive crosser**

   More tortoise than hare in your approach. You value moving through your changes one step at a time in a methodical way. You won't be rushed or corralled into action unless it sits right with your spirit and in the logical order you've mapped out.

   Could this be looking back at the Ladder exercise in Chapter 6 (see pages 91–2), mapping out your goals or rungs and taking the first step on rung number one?

3. **Enthusiastic crosser**

   This individual is ready to jump with gusto and be daring, bold and open to whichever way the wind blows.

   Perhaps you've handed in your notice, set up three very different experiments from your Ideas Lab exercise in Chapter 8 (see page 141) and you are seeing a clear winner.

There's no right or wrong here; my goal is for you to make a start TODAY.

Stay curious and open

The fact that you are reading this book means that you are at least a bit curious about what alternative routes your work happiness could take and are open to the magic that might unfold. That fire in your stomach will serve you well as we move into one of the pivotal sections of the book, embarking on the path to loving what you do! Yes, goddammit, the juice you've been waiting for!

I'm so excited to see how you will use what you've learned so far to make more empowered work-happiness decisions. Good luck, I'm rooting for you!

Visit www.loveitleaveit.co for additional resources, tools, templates and book recommendations for this section.

SECTION 4:

THE PATH TO LOVING WHAT YOU DO

CHAPTER 7

CAN I REALLY FALL IN LOVE WITH MY JOB?

What is it like to be in love? Most people will say there is the fuzzy haze at the beginning and lots of happy visions of future coupledom. After a while, the novelty wears off, you start to argue and you end up wondering whether this person or relationship is really worth all the hassle. Then you have to decide whether you want to work through the rocky patch or whether walking away is much better for your sanity. Much like any relationship, you will ride similar waves with your job over the course of your career.

I'm guessing most of you don't want to just *settle*. It's my aim in this chapter to help those of you who want to work through this crisis point in your work happiness because you know that your current company or role is taking you in the right direction. When you start to understand how to react better to certain people, challenges and situations, you can grasp ways to fall in love with your job before you bail out on the relationship entirely.

OK, let's get started on this journey of love!

I love my job but...

If you are in this camp, the chances are that you like your job, but there is still an itch that needs to be scratched. It's like a piece of vintage clothing that you've fallen in love with, but the fit is just slightly off. With a little nip and tuck here and there and a good clean, it's good to go.

I'm going to throw out a few 'I love my job but...' scenarios and, as we move through this chapter and the next, I'll be supplying the remedies for each.

I love my job but...

- I'd like to build some better relationships or repair some fractured ones
- I feel like I've become stilted in my job. What's next for me?
- I think I could be getting more money or recognition for what I do
- I need to change my attitude so that I can view it with a more positive mindset
- Something doesn't feel right. I like the pace and flow of my work, but what else can I explore?
- What I do currently isn't my calling – it's not the thing I see myself doing forever

Loving your job again involves looking at the journey through both an external and internal lens. The first three factors on the list are external areas that require you to work with other people to reach a positive state. The last three require you to go deep internally to detect what else you can bring to the relationship. We will explore each of these differing perspectives and give you the tools to take the important steps forwards.

I love my job but... I'd like to build some better relationships or repair some fractured ones

Do you dread working with some tricky characters on your team? Is there someone you just don't know how to motivate and the fact that they are dragging their feet makes you tense? Do you wish you could find your voice and be heard by your manager or your team?

I've spoken before about the importance of work relationships. For us to achieve great connection and unity and feel we have purpose at work, we need to build great partnerships at work. Good working relationships provide:

- Assistance to question our challenges and find opportunities
- Invaluable cheerleading and honest critique
- Mirrors that highlight behaviours that you might need to develop, change or address, pushing you out of your comfort zone or showing you how to be more vocal about your needs

I love this quote by Abraham Lincoln: 'I don't like that man. I must get to know him better.' The easy thing to do when we don't get along or agree with someone is to write them off as a bad person. It's much harder, yet much more rewarding, to get to know someone like that and the experiences that have shaped their approach to work and life.

You are the constant in all your relationships. If you want the relationships around you to change, a good place to start is working on yourself first. I follow a few mantras that have kept me sane when working with other people, my clients and those on my team:

- **Bring your best positive energy.** Be aware of your blind spots, your own idiosyncrasies, and how they might be affecting or shaping your relationships. So, for example, a big blind spot is 'treating commitments casually'. Maybe you are a bit of a flake, never fully delivering on time, always late and making casual promises you have no intention of keeping. When people are wary of your word, their relationship with you takes a low priority and you become immediately discredited.

- **See the whole person.** Learn to become an expert on emotional and non-verbal cues. Relationships are built or broken on what we choose to read into what a person says and doesn't say, and what we reject or ignore. I discuss non-verbal cues in Chapter 9.

- **Choose adventure over complacency.** Be curious and take the time to be inquisitive about the other person. Relationships are synonymous with adventure so enjoy the journey, the dips and dives, the twists and turns. Focus on being interested versus being interesting. Ask about the goals and visions of the other person, bond over your commonalities and let go of your own agenda of what you might want to 'get' from them.

- **Sharing is caring.** Open up, be real and honest about yourself too. The more you share about what you love and your quirks and worries, the more it encourages people to be open with you. In the wise words of Brené Brown, research professor at the University of Houston, 'Vulnerability is the birthplace of innovation, creativity and change.'

- **Manage your emotions.** We aren't clones and there are differences between you and another person that will rub you up the wrong way. It's your responsibility to learn how you react when someone does or says something that triggers you emotionally. Maybe you lash out quickly but get over any upset fairly swiftly, or perhaps you let things simmer and fester without really addressing what's wrong. How you handle your emotions and the actions around it can make or break your relationships.

You might be thinking that all sounds great in theory, Samantha, but this morning I want to throttle my co-worker. Help! Don't worry. Let's look at two ways in which we are triggered by people in our workplace:

1. Working side by side with a colleague or with a bigger team on a project or task together.
2. The culture and politics that emerge in every office environment.

Cast your mind back to Chapter 4 where we looked at the various types of characters that make up your office or perhaps your team:

- Commander
- Navigator
- Pacifier
- Cautious

Instead of allowing the people in your work life to become a sticking point, arm yourself with the knowledge to make some real changes. Below is an outline of what happens when each distinct personality pairs up. Keep in mind that some people, including yourself, can be a mixture of multiple types.

Two Commanders

Eek, so both of you want the power and the glory here! It's like being at war with your twin, which can raise the temperature and the tension as you are both competing for success, and lead to arguments and conflict. Is there someone like this at work who always pushes your buttons? Are they always vying to outdo you? In order to play nice and get things done, you both need to know your boundaries, goals and the roles you need to take to reach the finish line. Having these clearly defined parameters means you won't be treading on each other's toes. This might look like having an initial conversation around what each of you will be in charge of, and why: 'I'd like to deliver on X and I believe you would excel working on Y. How does that work?' Having that baseline agreement from the beginning will temper any unnecessary tensions.

The Commander and the Navigator

Success means two different things for each of you and it can sometimes feel like you are reading different chapters of the same book. For the Navigator, the prize is in social connection and glory. For the Commander type, it's about meeting that target and smashing that business goal. They couldn't care less about people as long as they bend to their will to get the job done. Both are demanding of each other in ways that can't be satisfied but, like the scenario above, if they have clearly defined roles and outcomes, they can smooth out the kinks for success.

The Commander and the Pacifier

As we've seen before, the Commander is reliable and people can expect them to produce results consistently. They will walk all over the Pacifier because they hate having to tend to everyone's feelings and needs. It could be a tricky ride for this duo, but it just takes a little patience on both sides as they have a lot to learn from each other.

The Commander can help coax the Pacifier out of their shell to empower them to speak up for themselves and confidently take the lead. This is something the Commander does well, if a little too often. Commanders can use their interactions with Pacifiers to build their patience levels and develop a healthy respect for alternative and diverse solutions. The Pacifier will need to find their voice in this situation and be succinct and open with the Commander. Commanders understand the language of success and the Pacifier must explicitly speak to the results that can be achieved through a united and collaborated front. For the Commander it might be worth noting that success in this partnership will mean reining in your forthright tone slightly, or at least be polite in how you deliver your message.

The Commander and the Cautious

Boom! Want to smash your goals? This pairing is the perfect duo. Just don't expect them to be bosom buddies outside of work. The combination of controlled doggedness and careful analysis equals results, but both need to have a strong understanding of what motivates the other. If you find yourself working with a Commander and you are Cautious, be explicit that in order for you to be spurred into action you'll need some insight into the details and logical facts; order is your main squeeze and without it you are lost. The Commander must remember to be mindful of their bullish nature and be aware that some people need more evidence of proof of concept before charging off in one direction. If they fail to recognize this, the Cautious will simply regress and become more reserved, insular and disempowered by doubt, slowing down the time it takes to achieve the desired results a Commander seeks.

Two Navigators

Whoop, this is where the party is at! You are both inspired and driven by the need to create great relationships and good times for all. While you are busy playing connector, selling in ideas, organizing events or counselling/coaching those in need, you will both find it difficult to focus for long periods of time. In an environment with tight deadlines this duo will struggle unless the value of *why* they should focus is connected to a people-oriented strategy. Otherwise, they will both go round in circles for days.

The Navigator and the Pacifier

If there is one person that can keep the Navigator focused, it's this partner. In this situation, the Navigator will bring their people skills to ensure the relationship grows as tasks get completed. But after a while, the Pacifier may become a bit clingy because they are attracted, like bees to honey, to the Navigator's extrovertism and feisty attitude.

The Navigator and the Cautious

Opposites don't always attract but in your case, to get sh*t done, you work well. One (the Navigator) is all about the affairs of the mind and heart and the other (the Cautious) is logical and practical. This equals fabulous results on projects, pitches and brainstorming sessions, but you'll have to be patient to forge a relationship beyond work. One is an extrovert and the other is insular and private and can't be forced to do anything until the time is right.

Two Pacifiers

Ah, aren't you both a dream? Well kinda... You are loyal, pragmatic, calm and intuitive. You both love to have time and space to come up with solutions, bright ideas and strategies, but that's the problem. Together you could both be planning indefinitely without any concerted action. Unless you are skillfully managed by someone else to meet an endpoint, it may be a very long time before an end is in sight.

The Pacifier and the Cautious

You may work well with a Cautious individual. But, if you are the Pacifier in this duo, what might irk you is the desire to connect on a personal level. Frankly it's not gonna happen, so you have to make peace with that or else. From the Cautious point of view, emotions and growing interpersonal connections get in the way of working efficiently. You just want to get your head down. But there is a beauty in lightening your load and allowing a Pacifier to get to know you. An old African proverb states that if you want to go fast, go alone; if you want to go far, go together. After all, Pacifiers are concerned with seeing everyone around them flourish, so let them assist you in the smallest way.

Two Cautious types

There will be competition between the two of you when there is an opportunity to show off your expertise to your manager or work on a project with your team. Each of you will try to outwit each other to come out on top and be crowned the best. But if you can both realize that two heads are better than one, then it's a win-win for everyone.

Let's look back at Tanya from Chapter 6, struggling to manage her never-ending workflow. On her team, she realized that she was in a sandwich between a Pacifier and a Commander. Her Pacifier assistant hated having to work to a timeline, so would spend more time than necessary finessing the finer details, whereas her other Commander assistant would zip through tasks with a very bullish nature, something Tanya longed to develop herself especially when her to-do list never seemed to end. With this insight, the three of them sat down to discuss better work practices, set up some accountability for all and allow her to keep everyone aligned and on track consistently.

Sometimes we are quick to brand others as being disruptive, laissez-faire or indecisive. We complain about it without thinking about the role we play too and what can be done to create the change we wish to see. A while ago, a coach told me that we have the power to train others in how we want to be treated. It does mean that we need to educate ourselves in our quirks first and know what our gut reactions are when our back is against the proverbial wall. Perhaps, as a manager, you can see why some of your team might be floundering and how, with a few slight tweaks in your communication, you can impact the behaviour of others.

Either way, I hope that you can slowly start to unpick the web of some of the behaviours in your co-worker relationships. When we hear a complaint or discontent, we can be triggered. Some of us shut down. Some want to complain back. Others try to smile or manage it away with niceties. The fact is that behind every action, argument or complaint is a hidden need or agenda that hasn't been fulfilled. We have to take a step back and do some digging to find the other person's perspective and the meaning behind their behaviour. We need to ask: 'What's going on here for you?', then take the time to listen and identify what need they are trying to express.

Side-stepping office politics

What if it's not just one individual but the vibe of the whole office that makes you a little ruffled? No matter what your office looks like, whether you are working in a plush office in the city or behind the counter at a department store, where there are people, there are politics.

Scan the landscape. Take a moment to observe the structure and the vibe of the office.

- Who has authority, but tends not to exercise it?
- Who are the real influencers?
- Who is respected by all?
- Who champions or mentors others?
- Who is the real brains behind the innovations and strategy?

Office politics often moves beyond traditional title hierarchy structure, so by asking yourself these questions you will have a real clue about where the power sits.

Unpick the connections. Now that you've narrowed down some of the power players, it's time to decipher how and why certain social networks and relationships are formed. How are some relationships built and maintained? Which managers are kept out or sit on the periphery of senior leadership decisions? What connections are based on friendship, respect, romance, or something else? It will help you understand why certain projects are given first to key members on your team or how influence flows between various departments or teams – and where you can operate to gain and build trust.

Get personal. Now you've mapped out the office landscape, it's time to build a diverse mix of relationships for yourself. While it's great to start with your own team, I want you to think bigger here. Think about managers or senior leaders in other areas. Networking isn't a game of take, take, take. It's about reciprocal growth. Get to know these individuals, their quirks, what you can do to help their growth and do your best to never break their trust. As you build your network be sure to create a mix of:

- Influencers – those who can have power to get things done, bypass traditional hierarchy and make things happen
- Connectors – consider your most important career and leadership goals
- Advocates – people who will speak highly of you when you aren't in the room

(Check out Chapter 11 (pages 201–26) where we delve more into how to build your network of mentors, connectors and advocates.)

Feed your network. After you've spent time nurturing and building your crew, you've got to start showing them where you shine. When you communicate your achievements to your connections, it's like a ripple effect in that they may open up new opportunities for you to shine and take on new responsibilities for you and those around you, including your team and your boss. Or they may act as a 'bridge' between you and other influential people too. For example, in a podcast with Bozama Saint John, chief marketing officer at entertainment agency William Morris Endeavor, she mentions including a section in her weekly meeting with her boss called 'Personal'. Here, she tells him about the amazing things she's pulled off that week, references interactions she has had with people he knows who were complimentary about her and finally what she wants to achieve and the help she needs to get there. Her point is that if you don't, who will? Doing this keeps him and a wider network of people up to date on her phenomenal work and keeps her at the top of people's minds for referrals, bonuses, connections and new projects.

Regulate yourself. Be brave but keep your wits about you. It's easy to let office politics grind you down and be sucked in by the negativity. First, avoid passing on gossip without carefully considering the source, credibility and impact. Nothing is ever totally confidential and assume that whatever you say will be repeated, so choose carefully what 'secrets' you confess or sides you take. If you're voicing your own worry, be composed and positive, but not aggressive. But when you have your own agenda and plan, all this other chit-chat is like water off a duck's back. If you feel like you want to scream, reflect on your emotions, what prompts them and how you handle them. If you can learn to self-regulate, you'll be able to think before you act and avoid saying something you might regret later.

Be the change you wish to see. You do have the power to change the company culture from within. Company culture, like any culture, is always moving and evolving. Instead of being passive and reacting to it, you need to realize you have the power to make people happier and influence those around you too. In the powerful words of Michelle Obama, 'when they go low, we go high'. Instead of getting sucked into belittling others, think of great ways to praise others, build better relationships on your team and be empathetic to your co-workers. Check out Appendix III (see page 253) to find out how you can create more happiness at work.

I love my job, but... I feel like I've become stilted in my job. What's next for me?

Job, career, calling. Which are you working with?

The job

Perhaps you need to stay in the job for a set amount of time while your partner irons out a new freelance gig or you test out a new business idea, pay off a debt or save? Or perhaps you are in this job to escape from another? It's an easy bread-and-butter gig to give you some healthy breathing space while you think about your future and make MONEY!

The career

You've been plotting your ascent in the company for a while and you are on a mission. You want more by way of money, a better title, that corner office, recognition, status or respect. Whatever it is, you are invested in making sure you get it and right now you feel a bit uncertain about how to secure your next leap. You might need to shift departments, reposition your role or test some projects within your current department. Are you ready and willing? Hang tight, I've got you!

The calling

A typical example of this is my client, Anthony, who dreams of directing and writing films that tell stories of marginalized and disenfranchised communities across the globe. He eats, breathes and sleeps this vision every day. Whether it's making short films for film festivals and competitions or sharing small activism videos on his Instagram page, his hope is that his films open the audience's eyes and can be a conduit to providing knowledge, ideas and awareness. Maybe you have a vision of crafting out a road to your calling in your current company and possibly you'd rather do it in an environment you know already than navigating it on your own for now.

Meaning, purpose and vision are all buzzwords associated with the young Gen Z (born before 1995) and Millennials (born between 1980 and 2000) who are the generations shaping and sculpting the parameters of what the future of work can be. Gen X (born between 1960 and 1980) and those older who've been in jobs for long periods are waking up to the fact that they can rejig a few things to boost job satisfaction. We are living longer and, as Lynda Gratton and Andrew Scott assert in their book *The 100-Year Life*, we need a different attitude to the role that work will play in the next third or fourth chapter of our lives.

Organizations are realizing that they need to be open to allowing employees to proactively tweak their roles and responsibilities to bring more engagement and meaning and, ultimately, to stay and be productive. It's up to you to articulate what you need to perform better and reinvigorate your tired role.

It's useful to address what your reasons are for wanting to reshape your job.

Motivation

What's your motive? Is it to build more contacts and friendships, fun, personal growth or secure a new job title? Do you want to grow your network and build a list of influential people who can put in a good word for you around promotion time?

Passions

Do you want to pursue some of your passions? An example of this is if you loved to see how things were made and spent your childhood taking electronics and toys apart and then putting them together again. This passion is being ignited further by a desire to move into engineering or robotic design.

Strengths

Do you want to leverage more untapped strengths? Use your natural ability to problem-solve, research and strategize. Perhaps you want to be included in more new product development meetings to exercise your creativity muscles further.

Take a moment and jot down your thoughts. Why does this matter to you?

....

....

....

....

....

....

....

If you don't do this now, the rest of your efforts will be futile. It will also be a colossal waste of time for everyone else you work with if you don't know why you are driven to make this change.

Now we can look at several techniques you can use to craft your job.

The building blocks of your day-to-day work

What are the tasks that you perform every day at work that make up your job? Consider how much time you are dedicating to each of the tasks or responsibilities and how they each make up your role. Can you see how your work becomes the building block for someone else on your team? What are the skills and strengths that you are utilizing across each task?

EXERCISE

Where does the time go?

Your first exercise is to map out the key tasks that constitute your working day. What day-to-day tasks do you have to do? What strengths are you playing to? How long do you spend on each task across the week? This will help you to know whether you are spending most of your time on what you love, what room you might have to add new skills to keep you indispensable and what you can start to delegate where possible.

Here I give you two separate examples: Kimberley who works in Marketing and Piero who works in a cafe.

Tasks	Time spent	Strengths/skills used?
Writing up a report of a social media campaign for client.	1.5 hours every Friday	Analytical, critical thinking, communicating
Restocking the drinks fridge and checking the sell-by dates on products.	30 minutes daily	Organizing

You can start to shapeshift your role when it comes to the tasks in the following ways:

- If you've identified space to learn a new skill in your working week, you can rejig your job by adding in a new task. Perhaps you've been keen to learn 3D modelling to showcase how the apartments you sell can come to life for your prospective buyers. Supercharging your sales role with these abilities helps your customer but also combines your passion for tech, design and sales.
- Create a prototype project. Perhaps there is another area of the company that intrigues you? Maybe you could propose a potential project between yourself and another individual in that department that could be a great cross-pollination of your skills as well as benefit the company or stretch their thinking around a customer problem. Who do you know who might be up for potentially collaborating or co-creating a prototype project?
- Emphasizing tasks. Take an existing task that you love and lean more into that – maybe building better customer and client relationships and less analysis of market data to lead to product ideas.
- Delegate. Are you spending too long writing lengthy reports and not enough time checking in with your team? If you do feel constrained by some of your tasks, how could you increase your delegation to make sure you are maximizing the full potential of your team?

Start today! Think about how you could craft your role by redistributing time or effort to different tasks, adding or deleting tasks or tweaking and altering tasks.

Building new relationships

As a Happiness Consultant, I've taken up the mantle to start a revolution around happiness at work. I help leaders and the HR of companies to design happier workplaces and cultures that support their employees. I created four pillars of happiness to help each company identify where they sit on the happiness scale:

1. **Head and heart.** These are traits around resilience, confidence and tenacity as well as problem-solving skills. How is the company equipping employees to bounce back from adversity and give them the autonomy to do it on their terms?

2. **Work and life.** What can the company do to reframe the processes and structures that may be inhibiting collaboration? Flexible working and office arrangements are part of this pillar. Another component is work-life harmony – how can employees learn to reflect on the compromises that are made to allow them to stay happy, even if not all the typical work-life balance boxes are ticked?

3. **Communicate and connect.** How can employees build better relationships with others? Where do communication breakdowns originate that make life in the office difficult and unpleasant? This pillar is often an area with a lot of problems. Most employees are frustrated by broken lines of communication and want to find more ways to connect. Unlocking the opportunity to create more connections, widen your social circle and learn more about what others do could help you to find more meaning in your work.

4. **Digital and mindful.** How does technology impact happiness and wellbeing at work? How can the company help employees find the balance between mindfulness practices and nature versus constant tech stimulation and distractions?

We can trigger new channels for communication by building and reframing our relationships. One of my clients Adrian, a web developer, was sick of being thought of as an 'introverted coder' like the rest of his team. He didn't find joy in sitting all day with his headphones on, churning out code. While he loved his job, he was intrigued by what other departments were up to and wanted to meet new people. He barely knew half the new joiners and, while the social events were nice, they were often unstructured and fleeting. He wanted to find ways to be a more integral member of the company and showcase his personality. So, with his line manager, we set aside time for him to get to know other teams and functions of the business with the end goal of working with HR to become part of the welcoming committee for the company. He would be one of the first ports of call for new joiners, give them a tour of the office, fill them in on each department and help them settle in. He helped to plan events and opportunities for teams to connect and build better relationships.

In this instance, forging deeper connections with people across all parts of the company increased his sense of belonging and worth beyond his day-to-day tasks. He was also able to reframe his relationships so that they were more than just buddies to go drinking with but individuals with multifaceted lives, awesome skills to contribute and interests that blew his mind. Lastly, he was able to share all this insight with key new joiners to provide valuable mentoring and coaching where he could. All while still creating some badass code.

What relationships would you like to build beyond your role? Which interactions would you like to foster? How can you serve someone or help to problem-solve for someone in a completely different department to you? Maybe you fancy nurturing the new intern you see in your department who is flagging under the weight of expectations?

I love my job, but... I think I could be getting more money or recognition for what I do

---

'Meaning and purpose feeds the mind but money feeds the stomach.'

Jenny Garrett, coach and trainer

I always ask my clients what an extra £5,000, £10,000 or even £15,000 would be worth in the grand scheme of things?

- Would it mean that you'd actually feel validated and a sense of recognition?
- Would it give you the confidence to know that you can pay your bills on time and start saving?
- Would you be able to take the burden off your loved one who may be picking up the financial slack at home?

Why do so many of us stick with the same old, same old? I'm often told:

- 'I just assumed that when the time was right, I'd get a pay rise.'
- 'The economy isn't great/my sector has been hard hit/we are a start-up with tight budgets/I'm lucky to have a job.'
- 'I haven't been there as long as others. Do I have the right?'
- 'I can't negotiate. I'm no good at it.'
- 'If I work harder, surely my boss will notice this. I don't need to ask'

This is all BS. When a company values you and you perform, provide value for others, innovate, deliver results and are an asset to your team, an extra £5,000–10,000 is nothing. If you say some of the above statements to yourself, this is really your inner gremlin at work stopping you from asking for your value/worth.

Taking control of your career means that you have to stop waiting for others to notice you and get proactive. If you know that you are a badass in your role, why aren't you getting what you are worth? Even in a tricky economic time, companies will go above and beyond to find the resources to retain top employees.

It's not risky to negotiate, it's stupid not to, but I continue to see women struggle here more than men. When you choose to stick with what you are given, you get stuck in the vortex of just accepting crumbs over the whole cake. Why should your manager stretch themselves to make it happen for you if you don't even want it?

Your employer has already spent a lot to get you onside: welcoming sessions, training and so on. Why would they want to flush that down the drain and start afresh with someone new? If you are ready to negotiate your pay, follow my steps.

Understand your worth and put a figure on what you do

Most people expect to walk up to their manager and get a pay rise on the spot. The minute you expect, demand or try to convince someone on the spot that you need a pay rise, you will be met with resistance and an instant no. The most effective way to get a pay rise is to do your planning.

Proper planning prevents piss-poor performance... Your coveted pay rise may require a one-to-six-month lead time depending on the size and type of company you work in, the number of levels of people you need to win over or communicate with, and the prep work you may or may not need to put in. But, from seedling idea to taking action and getting a yes, be open to this period of time as your baseline.

Stage 1: Before your first conversation (0–4 weeks)

1. Spend up to 4 weeks building your case and doing your research. Use sites such as payscale.com, salary.com, glassdoor.com, getraised.com to identify what a position like yours can earn.

2. Evaluate your earning potential – look at your skills compared to the average, years of service, education, extra training in relation to your job location, sector and so on. What is your case?

3. Look at the financial health of your company. Are you in a start-up without investor funding? Has the company just merged or been acquired? Have there been massive client losses? You can't always gain an idea of financial health from what you see, so do some digging of your own to get to grips with exactly where the company sits and what may or may not lie ahead. Even if you realize the company might not be in the best financial health, highlighting the value you bring to the company is always beneficial especially if they are thinking of making redundancies. While you may not in this instance achieve the figure you want, companies always want to keep top performers, even in lean times.

4. What is your company's existing pay review and progression strategy? Is there room for manoeuvre? The tech sector is constantly reinventing what career progression paths look like for creatives, developers, strategists and managers. Companies making great innovations are new start-ups like Monzo (mobile banking) and Buffer (social media scheduling tech company).

5. There are likely to be several types of questions circling your boss's mind whenever there is a money conversation to be had.

   - Am I worried about losing this person? *To be honest, we could do with streamlining the team. They have not really contributed much in the last nine months.*
   - Does this person deserve the salary she or he is asking for? *They are a great asset to the team morale and their ideas are genius. They always deliver and we can't do it without them.*
   - Do I have the money to say yes to this request? *We've had a dry period, pay rises aren't on the cards, but we can offer other things like training, personal development, etc.*
   - What would this mean for other people's salaries? *Is everyone on the team going to start asking for more money now?*
   - What's likely to happen if I say no? *Damn, is this person about to jump ship? I thought they were happy!*

It's worth keeping some of these questions in mind and preparing yourself as much as possible.

Stage 2: The first conversation

After your initial preparation and research phase, it's now time to speak to your boss or manager.

1. Set up a meeting with your manager to address how you can take your work to the next level. DO NOT MENTION PAY YET. Address what you love about your work, your current status and abilities and that you are keen to take yourself to the next level.

- 'I'm really enjoying/working on/doing X'
- 'Since I've been in my role, I've contributed/delivered on/set up/sold' (Showcase your skills, abilities, wins and achievements)
- 'I've been taking on more seniority in this role and delivering consistently on ABC'

2. You can see that the company could benefit from XYZ (gaps you've identified, areas where the company can outsmart competitors) and you want to do what you can to get there.

3. With all your data and research, you are now ready for the next phase of this initial conversation, which is to discuss your salary. Say 'I've been doing my research and for my role, experience, X, I think that I am being underpaid. I should be on X. I really enjoy working here but I would like a salary adjustment that works for us all.' Don't make it personal or confrontational with your boss. Show your research.

4. Explain the reason you deserve it. For example, 'Based on X I should be paid X per cent or an extra £X more.' Then be silent. Let your manager step in. It may go one of two ways:

   - 'Great let's discuss this further'
   - 'We are stretched. There are no funds. The economy is tricky.'

5. Most people will be put off by the second point and accept the status quo. It's important to highlight here that you are not being paid the average or the same as your co-worker and you are beyond average. Again, wait for your manager to say something here. It's not your place to take the economy as an excuse. It's your employer's role to keep you compensated if you are delivering. Stand your ground.

6. If your manager says yes, let's discuss:

   - An immediate increase to the average
   - Ways to work towards achieving this and the next level beyond just the average

7. If the second point is the focus by the end of this first meeting, agree 3–4 quantifiable goals with your manager. These are goals that require proof, for example, delivery of the gaps you identified, increasing sales by 15 per cent, converting/upselling new business for 3 clients or increasing podcast listeners by X. Whatever your role or job is, find out what 3–4 key goals you could work towards over a 3–6-month period to take you to the next level. If you achieve these goals, get your manager to sign off that you will be eligible for a salary increase on hitting these goals.

Stage 3: Getting to the next level and subsequent meetings (1–3 months)

This is the next stage after your meeting with your boss. If you have set some goals you are now in the process of working towards this:

1. Over the next three months, aim to exceed expectations and check in regularly. Make a habit of updating your boss fortnightly on your wins/progress/new business and so on. Keep your goals as a priority and cut out all the dead weight that keeps you busy but not productive. Email is one of them (other people's agendas) and disruptions from colleagues. Stay focused on your goals.

2. If you are having problems achieving one of your goals, be honest with your boss. 'I've found this online course which will help me be able to do more of X. Can I take it in order to reach my goals?' Keep them updated all the time on your progress and where you are exceeding expectations.

Stage 4: Sealing the deal (month 3 onwards)

You've been putting in the hard graft, now is the time for the win. Once you have completed your goals, set up another formal meeting to discuss them. Showcase how you have gone from A to B to C. Your manager should already be aware of your progress if you have been checking in regularly. Now is the time to state the improvements or progress you've made, the revenue you've generated for the business or the number of new customers. It should be no surprise to your manager that a pay rise is due as expectations and goals have been met.

I'm a bag of nerves... help!

It's only natural to feel nervous about talking to your manager, but the fact that you are taking this step is the main thing. All the work we did before on assessing behaviour traits at work will come in useful now. I'm not asking you to do any Jedi mind tricks, but it helps to know the behavioural attributes that your manager exhibits. What do they need to make decisions? How do they deal with direct dialogue? It's important that you keep your composure, be clear on what value you bring to the company and take all emotion out of it. If you have done your homework, there is no need to feel worried.

Avoid making it all about you and your needs when the nerves hit. Comments like 'I'm trying to buy a house so I need X', 'I'm struggling with living on...' might fly with some bosses, but not with others. Keep your language positive, future-focused and company-orientated. Show your deep insights into the industry, the company's positioning and where you sit in taking them from A to B.

No doesn't mean *no* in all cases

I think it's important to not get sidetracked by external forces that are the concern of the business, not yours. Being fairly compensated is a right. Ask your manager if the situation will change over the next few months and get it in writing that you will be eligible after, say, six months. What else would you be willing to accept beyond money in this interim period? How about training, additional perks or extended leave? Don't just walk away.

It's important, however, to be realistic. Have you put in the work to warrant your raise? Have you done the planning? If you have and are still coming up short, evaluate if you need to move on elsewhere to be better valued.

Rekindling the romance

You've taken a long hard look at the people in your office, the money you make and the job itself. It's easy to look at just the external trappings of love and base a decision on that, but it takes two to tango and in the next chapter we will be looking at your role in this love dynamic.

CHAPTER 8

IT'S NOT YOU, IT'S ME

We've discussed some of the external aspects that you can work on to supercharge your work happiness. Now it's time to shine a light on the internal nuts and bolts of your mind and inject some play and experimentation to help you keep that loving feeling going.

I love my job but… I need to change my attitude so that I can view it with a more positive mindset

Your partner can sometimes be your roomie, best friend and co-parent as well as your lover. You know their patterns, they know how you like your eggs and that you sleep in the same position every night. It's exactly the same with your job. You can smile and jest with your co-workers over lunch and smash your team targets like pros but, like any relationship, still feel like the magic is missing. Just as being stuck in a rut in your relationship can hold you back from becoming your full self, so can being stuck in a negative mindset at work.

What does it mean to have a positive, growth mindset? Carol S. Dweck, a psychologist at Stanford University, created the 'mindset theory' as a way to interpret the effects of the beliefs that individuals hold regarding their intelligence and their capacity to educate and learn new things. What does all this mean for us? In her book, *Mindset*, she describes how:

- If you have a *fixed mindset,* you believe that your intelligence, personality and skill capacity are set in stone. The day you were born, you are who you are and nothing can be improved, practised or developed further.
- On the other hand, with a *growth mindset,* you believe that effort or training can help you move mountains. Well, not literally, but the sky's the limit when it comes to enhancing your skills and intelligence.

Individuals with a fixed mindset tend to be interested only in feedback on their success in activities as it serves to evaluate their underlying ability. For them, success depends solely on the level of innate ability that they have. Failure is like a cosmic bomb because it just serves to highlight the upper limit of their ability and strengths.

The individual with a growth mindset welcomes failure with open arms. For them, it indicates where they need to pay attention, invest effort, apply time to practise and master a new learning opportunity. Like watering and caring for a plant, the more you attend to a growth mindset, the more it grows. The more effort put into acquiring new skills and knowledge, the more you can boost performance, attitude and success.

Time to shift gears

Have you noticed that your attitude and mindset are a bit uncompromising? Don't beat yourself up. We all have those moments when we become set in our ways, but you are in the right place to overcome this. Shifting gears on your work mindset means starting to:

- Identify how the mental changes you want to make will have repercussions on you and those who work around you. Whose help might you need to make sure you stay on the growth mindset path?
- Work out how you will build trust with others, so that they know you won't dump your work responsibilities if you find yourself overwhelmed with learning new things.
- Get active to create the change you want. Be progressive in mapping out the changes you want to make instead of waiting for opportunities to fall into your lap.

- ➤ Take small and frequent steps towards your goal, keep assessing what's working and what isn't, and adjust accordingly.
- ➤ Ask yourself what the bigger reach of your job is. Try to concoct a wider vision for your work that will assist in shifting your attitude and perspective. How might this alter how you engage with different activities in your working day? Is your work as a coder at an online academy working towards 'reinventing the MBA for the 21st century'? Some people would say I just offer workshops on career change. My perception is that I'm empowering a generation of people and companies to make work happiness a priority and create ripple effects on the wider culture, in communities and in people's lives.

Here are 22 ways to help bolster a positive, growth mindset and raise your work-happiness vibrations.

Helping others

1. Perhaps you want to start a running club or a lunchtime chess group. It's about bringing people together and taking the conversations beyond work.

2. Take a colleague out to lunch just because you feel that it is a nice way to make sure you both step away from your desk, get some fresh air and build some better bonds. This can really help, especially if this colleague is doing their best despite going through a tough time. Maybe they are a carer or perhaps their partner is unwell. A bit of compassion goes a long way.

3. Put together a game of coffee roulette for your team each month. Put everyone's name in a hat and a selection of random conversation starters in another hat. Each member has to pick out a name and talking point and then grab a quick coffee together to discuss the topic. This can be a great way to get to know people you don't normally talk to or to brainstorm a particular work problem. Possible starter questions could be:

   - ➤ What is the craziest, most outrageous thing you want to achieve?
   - ➤ Who had the biggest impact on the person you have become?

- If you had £2,000 to inject some new life into our department, what would you do?
- If you could learn the answer to one question about your future, what would the question be?
- Where is the most awe-inspiring place you have been?
- What do you do to get rid of stress?

4. Start a 'lunch and learn' session to encourage skills swapping or learning across departments.

5. Create a praise wall. It's a simple whiteboard or something similar that individuals can use to jot down mini achievements or praise for another person whenever the fancy takes them.

6. Start a book club or recipe swap club to share ideas and passions.

7. Turn dull meetings around by instigating a brief moment to meditate at the beginning and end to make sure people are attentive during the session and leave mindfully. Mix it up and suggest that phones are stacked in the corner, that there are no notebooks and nominate a different note-taker each time – or just record it – so that you are all just focused on problem-solving or discussing ideas without distractions.

Helping yourself

8. Make a list of your successes, positive client feedback, work wins or milestones achieved. When you're feeling down, remind yourself of the impact that your presence has on the wider company and how your skills and abilities are coming together successfully.

9. Invite the power of pause into your working day to embrace some stillness and connection with your breath. Whenever I feel like my back is against the wall or I'm having a slump, I take a moment to scan my body and focus on my breathing. I tried this while I was studying for my Gross National Happiness Facilitator qualification, learning about the Bhutanese philosophies and practices that promote happiness and wellbeing. Why not try the body scan exercise (see overleaf)?

EXERCISE

Body scan

- ➤ Find a comfortable position on a chair, close your eyes and tune into the posture of your body
- ➤ Try to keep your spine straight and energized, while relaxing the muscles around your skeleton
- ➤ As you breathe in, breathe energy and awareness into the spine, moving the spine gently upward
- ➤ As you exhale, feel yourself letting go of tension, stress and worry
- ➤ Be aware of the activity of your mind but let go of judgemental or critical thoughts when they arise
- ➤ Take each part of the body, from the feet to the head, and continue mindfully breathing energy and awareness into each area and releasing stress and tension

10. Monitor your moods, your health and your needs for greater productivity, focus and alleviating stress. Over the next decade there will be a rise of technology-based apps and innovations explicitly created to provide resilience throughout your working day, whether it's the Fitbit, which tracks every part of your day, including exercise, food, weight and sleep to help you keep fit, stay motivated and see how small steps make a big impact, or apps that allow you to meditate on the go like Headspace or Happy Not Perfect, by tracking your physical, mental and emotional wellbeing so you can identify what is helping and hindering you from being your best self at work.

11. Find a mentor – if you feel like you want to bounce some ideas or get some advice, it could be useful to find someone in another department who you admire or a person outside of work to discuss ideas with. (We will go deeper into this in Chapter 11.)

12. Teach as you do. There is beauty in sharing knowledge and perhaps there are some things you've learned through trial and error that

could shortcut someone else's learning. Maybe there's an intern who would jump at the chance to shadow you. If spreading knowledge or teaching others at work is a pleasure for you, let your endorphins soar.

13. Challenge yourself to go a day without complaining and find the beauty in what you do. Misery loves company and when we get stuck in complaining, others join in and it's a downward spiral. Every time you feel the urge to complain, think of one nice thing that's happened at work. If you do complain, stick a pound in a jar at the end of the day and see how much or little you've collected. If it's a lot, spend it on someone you care about.

14. If you've fallen into the trap of equating your work in terms of your monthly pay, why not look at the other benefits your company offers that go beyond salary. Have you sorted your pension yet? Does your employer match your contributions? Does your company run workshops on things like financial planning or food and nutrition? Do you have medical cover and does it cover things like seeing a therapist or acupuncture? Are there any opportunities to work remotely or take a sabbatical? Could you join a programme offered by Remote Year or Unsettled? These companies are booming at the moment, offering packaged experiences across cities around the world where you can join other individuals who are keen to explore living in a new culture and working remotely. If there are opportunities for a sabbatical, these are a great way to spend that time, exploring what makes you come alive, delving into new cultures and broadening your horizons. Could you take a month to do your job by the beach in Nicaragua or in the rice fields of Bali? Or could some downtime away exploring the bustling streets of Tokyo or trekking the Himalayas be the space you need to be re-energized again for your job? If these feel too expensive for now, what about staying where you are and using your time out from work to do some volunteering, online training or to learn a new language?

Educating others about what you need

15. At work you need to be able to articulate what you need and take responsibility for managing your mental wellbeing, happiness and general performance. This might include:

- ➤ Discussing upfront with your colleagues or clients your preferred method of communication and clarifying any relevant implications or changes to your working pattern
- ➤ Changes to your workspace, such as if you feel distracted by an open-plan office
- ➤ Finding help or requesting mediation if you are having a difficult time with a co-worker
- ➤ Learning how to say 'No' effectively if your energy and performance tank is running on empty; it's important to be assertive if you realize extra demands will diminish the quality of your work

Changing your work routines

16. Grab some plants. I can't tell you how introducing some little plant friends to my desk space has perked up my working day. It also works on my skills of patience and practice, making sure I remember to water, prune and take care of them.

17. Get yourself a mini diffuser. Mix up key essential oils like lavender, vetiver, rose or sandalwood for a calming effect on your moods. Other oils like lemon, basil, ginger and neroli can help keep you focused, energized and happier throughout the day.

18. Set up a colouring-book stand on your desk to aid relaxation or break up the monotony of tapping away on your keyboard. I've found it's a useful way to give my eyes a break from blue-screen hell and get my hands doing something different. A mini colouring break opens up my creativity and helps me feel energized.

19 Make creativity a habit. Think about one way to switch up your work routine at least two to three times a week. It might be taking a different route to work, rearranging your desk or hot desking.

20. Mihaly Csikszentmihalyi, a Hungarian-American psychologist, discovered that people find genuine satisfaction during a state of consciousness called flow. In this state, they are completely absorbed in an activity, especially an activity which involves their creative abilities. Music helps me get into flow and increases my work happiness. Why not create some focus or flow music playlists? I've got a Spotify playlist called Work Flow (original, I know). It never fails to get me into the work zone and keeps my mind from wandering off. As you've learned previously, I've got an Influencer vibe, so shiny distractions are constant curveballs I need to dodge. Great apps like Focus at Will create and curate music specifically based on your behaviour traits and neuroscientific data on what promotes the best in focus, productivity, efficiency and happiness, so you've got no excuse not to finish that report and stay in the zone to smash through your to-do list.

21. Are you sitting comfortably? Check your chair and lighting to make sure they are set up to help you work successfully without any pain or eye strain. Would it be possible to create a standing desk for a break from sitting? There's tons of research on the importance of good-quality light – it contributes to both efficiency and happiness.

22. Create a mini vision board of your work and life goals, which could consist of words, affirmations and pictures, and print it on an A5 postcard. My vision board sits on the wall opposite my desk and it serves as a timely reminder of my values, how I want to serve my clients in my business and how my work aligns to my life goals and desires.

This list is just the tip of the iceberg of how to create more loving feeling in your job – I could talk about this for days! However, if you visit www.loveitleaveit.co you can download a full Love It Action Plan and template to proactively help yourself at work as well as educate your line manager and colleagues on what you need to stay happy and mentally healthy at work.

I love my job, but… something doesn't feel right. I like the pace and flow of my work but what else can I explore?

You may find that your job is actually where you want to be right now, but that perhaps you are hitting a learning block or barrier. The work you do might keep you ticking over and productive but equally you might want to elevate your happiness by adopting some hobbies that have nothing to do with your 9–5 job.

Bring the mystery back

Coasting in a satisfactory 9–5 job is a double-edged sword. It's important not to get too comfortable for a variety of reasons. Nobody wants dead weight on their team, so you need to stay alert and be committed to adding value. Just as you can't expect your partner to be your be-all and end-all, your job can't always deliver your happiness. You may need to get some passions outside of your job to rekindle the love and zest for it. You've got to have a life beyond work so that you can come back refreshed and excited each time.

Out-of-office indulgences

Hobbies serve as boosts in ways we don't think of at first glance. How could your saxophone lessons help you tackle a client's PR strategy? What's the value in brushing up on your Spanish outside your accounting job?

We can spend a lot of wasted time processing an argument so that the issue just goes round and round in our heads keeping us up at night. The better solution is to step away from whatever we are stuck on and do something else. This is what's known as Combinatory Play, a term coined by Einstein. By taking the time to dabble in hobbies, random tasks or passions unrelated to the work, this act of opening up one mental channel by dabbling in another, as Einstein states, allows us to create space to power up new ideas, solve problems and shift attitudes. Light bulbs flash when we least expect it when we choose to play and divert our attention elsewhere. Obviously I'm not asking you to get up from your desk in the afternoon and grab a guitar, but if you are a freelancer or are working in an environment that has all kinds of distractions and toys, go ahead. I'm also not talking about doing the laundry when you should be writing your article – that's just procrastination.

What I'm alluding to is the kind of hobbies that can divert your attention, that can be difficult, fun, physical, enjoyable, intricate or just whimsical and done in the evenings or weekends. These serve a variety of purposes to help you fall in love with your work further.

John Ratey, professor of psychiatry at Harvard Medical School, spent much of his time studying how the brain is a malleable organ capable of development and change, and offering guidance on how to improve our lives. He suggests that we are born with neural pathways that keep us functioning – breathing, walking. Others are created by learning. When you throw yourself into a new hobby, your brain's neural pathways start to alter to improve productivity and performance. Professor Ratey states that when we choose to get disruptive, hack our problems and try new skills or practices, we can make new pathways for neurons to flow through. Choosing to take up hobbies beyond your realm of expertise keeps your brain nimble and you happier.

Hobbies also help you step out of your comfort zone, meet new people and adjust your perspective. Try something that tackles your inhibitions. Even if you hate meeting new people, there are ways to avoid small talk and still push your comfort threshold. Treat it like a game. What new thing can I learn about this stranger?

By learning a new hobby, you go through the four cycles of learning discovered by Noel Burch, an employee at Gordon Training International:

1. **Unconscious incompetence.** We don't know what we don't know. You have no idea how to master the skill or what it will take for you to do it.

2. **Conscious incompetence.** As you make a start, you are hit with the reality that you don't have a f**king clue. This is when we are aware of what we don't know and it can make us feel defeated and frustrated.

3. **Conscious competence.** You make tentative steps towards mastering the skill but it's not a smooth operation. There are lots of false starts and you are tentative. It's a bit like riding a bike for the first time.

4. **Unconscious competence.** You just flow. You've reached that peak point where it comes naturally to you, no thinking needed or any more tentative steps.

Allowing yourself to go through this cycle means that you will experience failure, excitement and doubt. These are all valuable experiences to help you become happier at work.

Being too close to your job means that you can't see the wood for the trees in other areas of your life. A bit of distance and mystery does wonders for any relationship. Whether you choose to start pottery classes, join foodie tours, attend talks on genetic engineering or make your own gin, make space for play. You don't know how it might shed new light on your skills and strengths.

I love my job but... what I do currently isn't my calling – it's not the thing I see myself doing forever

For some of you, your current job serves as a placeholder with a purpose for a set time period – increasing savings or paying off debt, easy hours that fit around your degree or training, gaining entry-level experience in a new industry or making contacts before taking the next leap to something else. Whether that is starting a new business, another job or a new direction with your advanced training, you are happy to ride out some heartache for a short period if you are clear on what you want or need from this relationship. However, some people I've met admit to being stuck in the 'in-between' job because they simply don't know what the next step is. This is a prime opportunity for you to get experimenting.

If you are feeling a bit lukewarm about your overall career direction but also don't have any concrete ideas about what's next, experimenting allows you to explore without pressure to make it a success straight away.

EXERCISE

The ideas lab

In Chapter 6 we talked about creating experiments to road test different ideas. If you are in a job right now that has set or manageable hours like a bar job, waiter or waitress, receptionist, telesales or cashier, for example, you can make the most of your 'off-duty' time to road-test your ideas.

Make an observation	Ask a question	Propose a hypothesis	Make a prediction	Test the prediction	Clarify
I hate serving coffee. The regulars are nice, but I can't do this barista job forever.	Things that make me happy are playing with the kids who come in with their parents, comic books, science fiction and making book/film recommendations to friends and customers. What would allow me the opportunity to do all these things in my working day/week?	Perhaps I need to move into a role connected to writing, books and children.	I wonder if I would be good at writing children's books. I need more practice. I should write more consistently. Maybe start a blog to find out. I should identify which authors I want to emulate and learn more about their journeys. Where did they study or did they gain experience somewhere?	I'm going to start writing consistently for the next two months and see if it sticks. I will see if there are any courses I can take to boost my story development skills. Do I prefer writing or curating and recommending titles? I might start a book club around science fiction books for young teens to find out.	After two months of writing I realized that I have more passion for this than running a book club. I want to keep exploring further and maybe get some work experience one day a week. I can reduce my hours to do this.

In my earlier work I was so frustrated by what I was doing that I was chasing my tail. When I started taking classes in fashion and footwear design, my mind got the freedom to play and be creative. My self-confidence blossomed, my shyness dissipated and I made a new network of relationships. Clearly I didn't end up launching my semi-bespoke footwear line (not yet anyway) but it was the springboard into working with individuals and finding the match that lit my fire.

Can you love it enough to work it out?

There is much to be learned from being in a job you love but struggle with. For example:

Resilience – the ability to bounce back from obstacles or challenges.

Persistence – trying or pursuing a direction if you believe what you are trying to create is worth it, or the empowered feeling that comes from grasping skills that were previously out of reach.

The ability to bolster underused strengths – being in a tricky situation allows you to build new strengths you never knew you had, such as becoming better at rapport-building.

Building relationships for life and making new friends with diverse people different from your current social circle.

Take stock with a friend of where the pros and cons are in your plan to be happier at work. I've given you some practical steps to help you to transform your love for your job. You just have to take action with what resonates most.

'Better a diamond with a flaw than a pebble without.'

Confucius

Obviously, a job you don't enjoy or wholeheartedly love is very different to one that is damaging your health, super toxic or standing in the way of your bright new business idea. But, all too often, we can be quick to run from one job to another that looks glossy from the outside but is far from it in reality. The new job may end up having other flaws too which will show up in time.

If you have reached a point where you can't find the love, remember that there's no shame in walking away. In fact, you'll do yourself a favour by giving yourself a chance to find what's right for you and you'll give your employer the opportunity to find someone who would love your role more than you do.

Next we look at what happens when leaving is the only real choice on the table. Don't be scared. On the other side of your fear are two exhilarating 'Leave It' pathways towards work happiness.

SECTION 5:

WHEN YOU'VE LOST THAT LOVING FEELING

CHAPTER 9

IT'S TIME TO JUMP SHIP

We've spent some time looking at how to fall in love with work, but you might now be thinking one of a few things:

- ➤ That's all well and good, Samantha, but realistically, another minute in this job and I'm going to scream
- ➤ I see where you are coming from, but something is still missing
- ➤ If I don't jump now, I will miss a great opportunity or a gap in the market

I'm going to give you an alternative roadmap that will help empower you to revolutionize your working life. It's all about elevating your levels of happiness. Where are you right now?

1. Are you currently in a toxic, demoralizing and stressful job? Ready to switch departments in a company you are enjoying being part of or to find a new job in a similar or burgeoning industry?
2. Or maybe you are ready to experiment with a portfolio career or road test that new business idea you are itching to investigate

I want you to think back to Chapter 4, where we deciphered the different types of work pain. Right now, you might be nodding your head, realizing that it's likely you are in toxic job, in which case you have to jump out of the fire ASAP. I say this because working in a toxic, stress-inducing job does nothing for your spirit. In fact, it stamps all over it, chews it up and spits it out, only to stamp all over it again.

I've seen it time and time again with clients who feel trapped and are itching and ready to move on. They are working day in, day out, in a job that doesn't feel right but by the time they get home from work they are exhausted, drained and fraught. This is totally the wrong energy to have when you are trying to visualize the new career or job you want.

In these cases I help clients work out if it's possible to find a straightforward sideways move into a similar job elsewhere with a better culture, more clear-cut hours and space to breathe. This might sound slightly strange. How could a horizontal move to another area in the same industry be helpful? Isn't it just more stress? But this action alone creates the space and time so you can actually craft and experiment to find your new career (think back to the Ideas Lab exercise in Chapter 8, see page 141) while finding some semblance of good mental and physical health, along with keeping your finances in check. Yes, it's easy to say that you should quit your job, but that's a massive action that could have disastrous repercussions. It's the sexy thing to do, but often it leaves people floundering with too much time on their hands and dwindling savings. I believe career change is about small, manageable and measured steps towards your ideal career.

Or maybe you want to keep your current job, but reduce your hours to attempt to build a portfolio career? Have you considered creating a business that works around you and your family or becoming a solopreneur with you at the helm of the business and no need for investors or big venture-capital funding? A portfolio career allows you the freedom to experiment and shapeshift your working hours to do more of what you love and leverage your skills.

We cover this in full in Chapter 10 but, for now, I'd like you to ponder the following:

- Imagine the opportunity to renegotiate the parameters of your working week in your current job and mix it up with some freelancing or testing out your favourite hobby to see if it's a money-maker

What new lease of life would this give you? You could think about working three or four days a week instead of five in your main job and growing your lifestyle business on the remaining days.

- Perhaps you've been dying to pair together two very different skills and passions that could bring in more money than your current job. For example, maybe you've wondered how your skills and passion for youth work, sales and food could work together. Now is your chance
- Or maybe you've found a co-founder for your latest business idea and, after numerous nights and weekends plotting and planning, you are both ready to go part-time in your jobs to drive it forward

The old job versus the new job

It's time to decipher just what kind of 'new job' you are looking for and whether or not you have to fully retire the 'old job' in its current guise. What do I mean by this? Well, I think there are three approaches we can take to 'Leave It' when it comes to finding a new job role:

1. Staying in your current company, but pivoting by switching job roles or departments: maybe the company you are in ticks all your boxes, but working in sales has lost the sparkle and there is an opportunity in the talent recruitment team that, with a bit more training, has your name all over it.

2. Moving into a new industry, but doing the same job and using the same skills: in this case it might be that your current job and skills can be revamped by jumping into a new industry. Technically, it's not a new job; instead it's had a makeover and reinvention due to the new company or industry. Maybe you are an IP lawyer moving from an independent boutique entertainment law firm to the legal department in a big multinational.

3. Moving industries and tackling a brand-new job: this is new squared, equalling a huge change.

With all these delectable options, I hope you are excited by the possibilities. I am!

In my journey doing this work, I've come across two types of people:

1. Those who have that little voice in their head that is clear about the next steps, but still don't make any moves until one conversation just tips them over the edge.

2. Others who sit in a whirl of confusion and paralysis until perhaps a little confirmation from their trusted circle pushes them to take the next step forward.

It's easy to think that career change is just a solo endeavour but it's not. 'Leave It' involves stepping out of your comfort zone: meeting and engaging with new people and tapping into your existing circle of friends, family and past and present co-workers to carve out your new routes to happiness.

So far, we've done a lot of solo soul-searching. This next exercise is going to help you get some insights into where you could shine a light further. The 'What should I do?' survey will help you get some clarity on where you are right now, what you are capable of and what you need to let go of to get there.

EXERCISE

What should I do?

Send these survey questions to 3–5 people – friends, family or colleagues – then sit back and see what you learn from their responses. Be brave – send it out to the people you know will help you. If you've already got a set vision, this exercise can help to solidify your thoughts.

- What do you think I'm the best in the world at?
- Which of my talents do you think I'd be doing the world a disservice if I continued to hide away?
- What do you think I need to let go of or overcome to find my desired career?
- In my next career do you think I should be .... ? (Examples include helping people, exploring outdoors, teaching others, building something, designing, leading others, investigating or problem-solving or getting physical.)
- On my deathbed, what do you think my biggest career regret would be?
- If you could create a job title for me or find an existing one, what would it be?

Jot down your notes in the space below:

....

....

....

....

....

....

The winner takes all...

The 'What should I do?' survey is great because it reminds you of your attributes, successes, strengths and aspirations that have been shiny and noticeable to those close to you.

You've got to be able to articulate your personality and what you can offer pretty quickly. I say this for two reasons:

1. Recruiters, HR and hiring managers are strangers to you. They don't have the background knowledge that your social circle and contacts have acquired over the years.

2. Coupled with this, depending on your culture or personality, you may not spend enough time talking about your achievements or successes. Perhaps it's seen as crass or you may perceive it to be self-indulgent. A lot of my clients struggle with this, modestly going about their day and not sharing their achievements.

In Chapter 8, one of the 22 ways you can boost a positive mindset is by making a list of your successes, positive client feedback, work wins or achieved milestones. I'm hoping you gave this a whirl? If you skipped that section, that's fine, but the next exercise is going to be a test of your memory. It will be worth it though.

EXERCISE

The success scoreboard

Ask yourself these questions to shape your expectations and get you ready to articulate your brilliance:

- What have you done in the last 6–12 months that has been a professional success for you, your team or company? (If you aren't currently in work, maybe look at your last role or the role before that.)
- How might you explain this success and the results achieved to someone who doesn't know your company or team or the related circumstances?
- At your current rate of work competency, can you expect a promotion or salary increase in the next six months if you stay where you are? If yes, why do you believe this? If not, what's affecting this?
- How aligned are your attitude, mindset and behaviour to positively influence your next career leap?

Together with your transferable skills and strengths toolkit from Chapter 5, these questions will help to build a wider picture of your experience. Getting clarity on what spice and magic you bring to a working environment will be pivotal in pitching yourself at interviews and meetings with potential HR managers or employers. Jot down your notes in the space below:

....

....

....

....

....

....

Do the work upfront first

Success doesn't happen overnight. It takes research, hustle and strategy to create the wins. It's important to get some insight into the industries and markets you want to move into before you start applying for a new job.

Looking at the market:

- What are the types of companies you want to apply to? *Are you drawn to start-ups? Big, solid, trusted brands or multinationals?*
- What job roles and responsibilities are you attracted to?
- What types of product and services do you want to work on?

It helps to think back to the B.R.I.D.G.E. exercises (see pages 39–44) and the Job Prescription exercise in Chapter 4 (see page 47).

By understanding all the interconnecting elements in your day-to-day working life, we can start to find out what can be fixed through your job move and therefore prevent the pain being repeated. Armed with this information, you can start to pinpoint what's available on the job market and how it compares to what you actually want. Mining the data like this helps you to identify what roles you might need to pitch yourself for.

Career fire-starter conversations

It's also time to start thinking about who are the right people to have career fire-starter conversations with over coffee (or, my favourite, a turmeric latte). These conversations aren't formal nor are they job interviews; they are moments for you to build relationships and gain the knowledge you need to devise your next move effectively.

Start by emailing your network with your insights about your desired career direction and how they might be able to help. By network, I mean friends, family, key professional contacts (ex-colleagues and schoolfriends) and any individuals you know who work or used to work in, or are connected to, your preferred companies.

EXERCISE

Your fire-starter approach

Below are a few tips on how to structure an initial approach letter or email:

1. A brief introduction, distilling where you are now, where you want to get to and why this shift feels important.
2. Your core strengths, skills and relevant professional achievements.
3. The ideal companies, industries and sector you want to progress to. The key changes you feel you can bring about for these specific companies.
4. How they can help you. Maybe it's connecting you to someone who you know is in their network, forwarding this email on, being mindful if they see opportunities arise or books or resources they think could be useful for you on this journey.
5. Sign off by thanking them and asking if there is anything you can do to help them by way of an exchange.

While this might sound pretty formal, feel free to phrase it differently when sending to family or friends. From this exercise, you'll hopefully start to get some recommendations or connections that could be beneficial for you to reach out to. It's important that you have a two-pronged approach so, alongside this, map out a list of individuals you don't yet know but need, whether it is:

- HR managers/founders/leaders of the companies you like/admire/ want to join at some point
- Employees within said companies with whom you can meet to get deep insights on the culture and job roles
- Identifying the hiring/talent managers and learning about what they are scouting for and what makes an ideal candidate

Because, let's be realistic, most CVs end up in the bin or lower down an email inbox. What puts you ahead in the race is:

- Building relationships with these gatekeepers – the people doing the hiring/recruiting, the HR managers, leaders and company founders
- Understanding their professional hopes, fears, needs, wants
- Pairing your skills against the problems they need solving
- Showing an interest without expectations

This is about ACTION. You do not get the work you love by hanging back and being chilled. Be bold, be brave and start to approach these people to get under the skin of what jobs are available, what you need to do to be considered and where you might be able to pitch yourself in the gaps you've noticed. You don't need to explore all of this in your first meeting, it might be over a series of conversations. But these are important discovery sessions to work out if this is where you should be moving to and whether you've got what it takes.

How visible are you?

While outreach is all well and good, you have to make sure that when these gatekeepers do their research on you, they can find out about you without difficulty and like what they see about your work story. In this day and age, your online profile is everything. How visible are you *and* your work endeavours? I'm not saying you need to be hanging out on Instagram, The Dots or LinkedIn every hour of the day, but what will potential employers learn about you when they type your name into Google?

I asked super-expert Bianca Miller-Cole about her tips for selling your skills and experience on LinkedIn. She's an award-winning entrepreneur, author, speaker, personal brand specialist and runner-up of the famed show, *The Apprentice*. In 2016, Bianca was awarded a prestigious 'Power Profile' by LinkedIn as one of the top 10 most powerful leaders on the website. She was chosen from 20 million members in the UK and is joined in this list by household names like Richard Branson, James Caan and David Cameron.

The fundamentals of LinkedIn

Picture: These tell a thousand stories. What does your current LinkedIn photo say about you? Do you look approachable, happy? Does it make you shine and clearly demonstrates the value you deliver? Can we see you clearly? Avoid distracting backgrounds and make it clear and engaging.

Name: Fairly obvious, but no nicknames here. It's worth noting if there are any recent changes. Have you just got married? Are people searching for you under your maiden name still?

Title: Bianca suggests titles should be made up of keywords that are memorable, representative of you and pithy. Keywords like 'Entrepreneur', 'Videographer, 'HR Director' allow you to be searchable but spell out quickly what you do. I prefer to go one step further and create a memorable title/work umbrella (more on this in Chapter 10). For example, 'Happiness Consultant'. It's an instant differentiator so that you stand out in the crowd.

Summary: This is your elevator pitch and can be written in the first or third person. Some people prefer to write in the third person as tooting your own horn can feel awkward. This should not be a dry list of your day-to-day responsibilities... snoozeville! Think of it as a discursive entry about what you can provide the world, whom you seek to work with or meet, what you want to achieve and why. For example, a psychology graduate ready for exciting opportunities in child psychology and development, with a keen interest and experience in attachment theory in under five-year-olds. Or an experienced designer and educator creating learning experiences for individuals, schools and businesses within areas such as technology, design thinking, communication, innovation, culture and entrepreneurship. In the summary section, consider the following:

- Significant career accomplishments: ones that are aligned to where you want to go. If you are looking for a job as a coder, stating that you were once an employee of the month at McDonald's is not relevant
- Your 'superpowers', passions and values (things you do better than anyone else). Remember all that good stuff we distilled in Chapter 5 – use that here
- Verifiable facts and statistics: what targets did you smash? How many customers did you convert? What audience sizes have you spoken to?
- Showcase any social proof via quotes and testimonials from clients, customers or recent press

Media: This section is for you to post your websites, blogs or showreels. This is a great space to direct people to videos showcasing more of your brilliance and skills. Videos are the best way for people to get a real sense of who you are and, in an age where audio and visual content is queen, you would be doing yourself a disservice if you ignored the opportunity here to flaunt yourself. If you haven't got any of your own content just yet, you can link to sites that you appear on.

Articles and activities: What have you got to say? Just like every other social media platform, there is an opportunity for you to share your views and opinions, to position yourself as a thought leader who has something to say. These don't necessarily have to be long- or short-form written pieces. With the inception of LinkedIn video, you can include short interviews, solo pieces to camera or snippets of you giving talks or demonstrating your craft.

Experiences: Here is where you get into the nitty gritty of what you've been spending your days doing. What jobs you've had, or work experience if you've just graduated. Use this space to discuss the accomplishments, results and wins you've achieved as opposed to tiresome long lists of day-to-day tasks. Again, it's about taking the reader on a journey, not sending someone to sleep with facts. It's helpful to show companies or interested parties what benefits you can add to their business.

Skills and endorsements: Listing your skills is a great way to show at first glance more of your magic. Whether it be coaching, venture-capital assistance, research or dentistry, these are surefire ways to ignite excitement in potential connections if they can see immediate synergies with what they are looking for. When others endorse you for this skill, it highlights to your wider network just how good you are.

Recommendations: These bring your profile to life. When your peers, mentors, old co-workers or former bosses wax lyrical about how awesome you are, this is a win. It saves you having to do all the hard work, so make sure you reach out to key individuals whom you think would be willing to share some gems.

Accomplishments:

- Projects: extra-curricular activities held while at university, maybe you were head of the Korean Film Society, or perhaps you started a magazine while in your current day job
- Contributions: speaker or panelist at a global conference

Rather than fear The Dots or LinkedIn, see them as your best allies to getting the job you want. The next exercise will help you dust down your online visibility, so that all the information online is consistent about you and sets the right tone for the future moves you wish to make.

For more tips on how to create a superstar CV and LinkedIn page, head to www.loveitleaveit.co to unlock more tips and resources.

EXERCISE

What's your work story?

The power to create the narrative of your work story is in your hands. Everyone now has access to various online platforms, whether that be LinkedIn, The Dots, Twitter or Instagram, to showcase their skills, personality or past work history. So it pays to take some time to make sure you are happy with what people might find when they start to research you.

- What happens when you or someone else googles you? What comes up?
- What does your LinkedIn profile say? Is it coherent about where you want to go or do you need to tweak it? If your profile talks about the amazing work you do as a Head Chef, but you want to move into coding and there is nothing else to suggest your experience around this, there is a disconnect.
- Do you have any other online presence that can support your new career direction? (Even a holding page with a domain name in your name stating your achievements, with a downloadable CV or video CV, listing awards, achievements, wins, an advertisement of yourself or some Ideas Lab experiments you have successfully completed, see page 141.)

Decoding the job advert

Your CV should be a mirror of the job advert itself. Ideally, it should be crafted to match the job advert in three ways to make sure you get a foot in the door:

1. Use the same words as the job advert.
2. Highlight the exact skills they required.
3. Focus on the value you can add in line with what they are describing.

As we move into a time where artificial intelligence is doing the picking and CV sorting, you may end up being rejected if you decide to stray off the path. Unless you match what they are looking for, you won't be seen to fit the mould. As this technology gets increasingly smarter, I'm sure this issue will be resolved, but for now just stick to the necessary and wait until the interview to show your flair.

Let's take a look at the position of Wellbeing Officer in the People & Culture department of a large corporation. Most jobs are broken down into three parts – a summary of what the role means for the company, what they want you to do to make it a reality and the skills they need to know you have to make sure the fit is perfect.

Job ad speak	Cutting through the bulls**t	Extra points to note
Job Summary • We believe revolutionary solutions can change the world for the better. • We are undergoing a period of groundbreaking change.	• The company is going through a period of exciting growth – it's a time where they need new ideas and fresh thinking around wellbeing to take them to the next stage of people development.	
• You will be assisting the evolution, execution and on-going management of an integrated Wellbeing strategy. You will be required to collaborate with various stakeholders across different departments.	• You must be able to take an idea from beginning to end, working and building relationships with people who all want a piece of the pie. Their opinions may well be opposing. Can you navigate the egos?	

Job ad speak	Cutting through the bulls**t	Extra points to note
You will be responsible for: • Co-ordinating and actioning the annual calendar of events to shine a light on key wellbeing issues.	• Managing multiple things – organizing events, relationship building, communication, data analysis.	• This is where digging deep and extracting the value from your current role in the exercises in Chapter 5 (the Skills Gap and Connecting the Dots, see pages 67–9 and 81–2) will help you flesh out and decode whether you have what it takes for the role. Equally it will be useful for you here to map out what transferable skills and work experience examples you can weave into your cover letter and potential interview answers.
• Exploring the most ingenious ways to correlate data against initiatives being run with the aim of demonstrating and increasing the impact of these internally, and, as a result, share best practice with the wider external community.	• Not wasting their money on running events that don't translate into positive results or changes.	
• Managing and creating best practice action-steps that highlight how to address Mental Health and Wellbeing from an employee and manager perspective, making sure they are up-to-date and being utilized as much as possible by various audiences.	• Aiding managers and employees to have difficult conversations about mental and physical wellbeing and helping, where necessary, to make sure they know the right lingo to use. This is where you need a diplomatic bone to make sure all parties feel heard and not offended.	
• Monitoring health and wellbeing trends.	• Keeping your eye on trends to make sure that the company is ahead of the curve when it comes to wellness. They said they were growing so there's no time for stagnant ideas here! If you aren't up to date with the latest and greatest innovations and don't love being an early adopter in your field, forget about it.	
• Managing relationships with external providers and with internal function.	• Balancing personalities, where everyone and anyone has got something to say.	

Job ad speak	Cutting through the bulls**t	Extra points to note
Experience and skills: • Previous experience with Wellbeing, Events and People & Culture. • Preparing, discussing and presenting materials. • Attention to detail and analytical skills. • Work in a team in a collaborative, supportive and open manner.	Nothing new here. • Essentially, are you able to use a computer, demonstrate that you can talk to people at all different levels, some of whom may or may not be invested in what you are trying to achieve, and persuade them to get on board while doing it in a quick and orderly manner? Can you also demonstrate past performance, successes and a passion for Wellbeing?	This is where the sea parts for men and women here. No sweeping generalizations, but I've seen it in the flesh! Women will look at the experience section and decide that they haven't got enough years doing XYZ and therefore don't apply. STOP IT! Just give it a whirl. Most men decide it's worth a punt and give it a try. Do the same!

EXERCISE

The CV makeover

Think about the jobs you want to apply for. How can you reword your CV based on what they are asking for and the knowledge you have gleaned from your fire-starter conversations (see pages 154–5)?

1. **Staying in your current company, but switching job roles or departments**
   Scenario: Essentially you love your company but have grown tired of working as an account executive and you want to move into copywriting.
   Strategy: Showcase how any extra-curricular activities have shaped and honed your interest in this new department or job role so that it doesn't seem like it's a whim. Maybe you have a blog or can write some copy as a trial for a new product.
2. **Moving into a new industry, but doing the same job with the same skills**
   Scenario: Working as a PR manager for a financial company has lost its appeal. You want to move into Hospitality and you are keen to handle the social media for luxury hotels instead.
   Strategy: Your CV needs to highlight why you are suited to this new arena and your cover letter needs to demonstrate why you want to make this shift and the value you can add.
3. **Moving industries and tackling a brand-new job**
   Scenario: Bored of being an architect, you are ready to develop your taste for high-end cuisine and cooking. You are willing to do what it takes to work in a top restaurant.
   Strategy: Highlight your transferable skills, wins and successes in your current department and/or role, and why you can and want to make this jump. What additional training have you undertaken and which past experiences have prepared you for this leap?

Your cover letter and CV should demonstrate initiative and, if you can show the hiring manager or recruiter how and why you can seamlessly fit into their organization, you've done them a favour. Let's be honest, these people are busy folks. You have to show them your worth and your determination and make it easy for them.

Interview time

You've been invited into the hot seat. Great! You might be tempted to use this opportunity to just talk, talk, talk about yourself. From the minute you walk into the interview, the judgement begins around your personality, your mannerisms, your attitude and your approach.

An interview is always both a two-way conversation and a delicate dance. I say dance because it's a balancing act of listening, observing and mirroring your interviewer's behaviour, and showing your personality at significant points.

You might think that these are all fairly easy things to do but when you get into the interview and nerves get the better of you, sometimes things fall through the net.

Listening

We would all like to think we listen fully to each other. But the reality is that more often than not we are only half-listening, often out of politeness and habit, and just picking up odd phrases that reconfirm what we think the other person is saying or trying to convey to us.

Instead of being caught up in our own thoughts, frantically problem-solving or formulating our next answer, what we need to do is to stay present and in the moment, open our minds and step into the other person's shoes (the interviewer in this scenario).

This means avoiding the desire to interrupt or jump in, but instead pace our responses in line with what we have actually heard.

- ➤ Show proof of listening by restating the key points you heard and ask whether they are accurate. 'Let me check that I heard you correctly…' is an easy way to clarify any confusion
- ➤ Provide regular feedback to the speaker, so they have some proof that you are listening and that you are following their train of thought
- ➤ Don't get queasy in the silences; we often want to fill silences with solutions, but there is nothing wrong with allowing pauses for you both to collect your thoughts

Observing

Much like listening, the art of really understanding the person sitting before us can mean that we have to become better at reading the non-verbal cues and signals that people give off.

Non-verbal communication is all the hard-to-grasp communication that happens between two people that's beyond words. So, in plain English, this encompasses body movement, posture, facial expressions (frequency of glances, rolling of the eyes and blinking), details of dress and pauses.

By appreciating non-verbal as well as verbal communication, we can pick up useful insights on how to respond better to others.

- Take the time to study their eyes without staring in an awkward fashion. Are they fixed on you when you speak or do they look distracted?
- What's the expression on their face? Is it welcoming, stern, detached, stressed or open perhaps?
- What are their head movements? Are they nodding in agreement or tilted with a perplexed vibe?
- Are there any mixed signals? A good example of this is when you explain your deep interest in a particular area of the job role while simultaneously having your arms folded firmly against your body, which suggests distance and resistance

Mirroring

This is done by subtly reflecting your interviewer. It's about cleverly adjusting your mood, posture, tone, word usage, language and actions to rhythmically mirror those used by your interviewer. Mirroring has the effect of stimulating trust and puts everyone at ease.

- Listen to their phrasing, language and sentence structure and try to recreate it but using your own unique language patterns; this isn't about mimicking the other person – it's about meeting them on the same playing field
- Only reflect positive speech and body language
- While it's crucial to notice the movements and mannerisms of your interviewer, you don't need to get caught into a vortex of doing this

so much so that you stop hearing what they're actually saying and forget how to respond. Yes, mirroring helps to establish rapport, but don't lose sight of what you are there to do – sell yourself and ultimately get the job

I caveat these techniques with the fact that each interview will have its own pace and rhythm. You need to be open to bobbing and weaving with your use of each of these different techniques. We can read the signs and mirror all we want, but a warm, kind and open interviewer does not always equal an impending job offer. Sorry.

Focusing on the company needs

While the interview is a time to present yourself in the best light, the ultimate action you need to focus on is making sure you can meet what the company needs and requires from hiring you. All of your rich conversations and research should give you an insight into where the company stands currently, what the struggles are and how your insights, together with your transferable skills, will help them succeed.

If you know you have strengths in technology and a passion for connecting people and building relationships, why not come up with three ways your skills and strengths could solve a glaring problem you've learned about from your conversations and research? What are they not seeing that you can solve for them? These are often great little anecdotes or ideas you can add to your cover letter or suggest in interviews. A word of caution here: it's important to be mindful of the tone and delivery of your suggestions. Don't be derogatory or come across as a know-it-all.

EXERCISE

The 'get-hired' equation

To give yourself the best shot at an interview, it pays to be one step ahead of the competition and show the interviewer your prowess in innovation. This exercise helps you to pair what you have to offer with the needs of the company and highlights to the company the benefits of hiring you to elevate their product, service or operation.

When you are asked to tell your story or explain why you applied for the job in an interview, pick out the key elements of your professional achievements that are relevant to what they desire and are looking for.

X + Y x Z = GET HIRED

My experience in X (sector/industry/job role) means I can bring Y (skills/strengths/knowledge) x my desire to help you meet Z (goals/agenda/targets/fill the gap) = GET HIRED

X – I've spent 10 years working in this field.
Y – I bring the best retail sales skills for dealing with various types of international customers.
Z – The impact of online shopping has meant decreased in-store customers, so you will need to create a better experience especially for international customers. I believe you can change this by doing ABC and I know Mandarin. I would help you raise sales by X per cent.

Here is an example from one of my clients: 'My experience in tech PR with brands like Xero and Etsy and then for my own start-up, means that I can distil and unpack these success strategies to help new tech brands achieve the same results on smaller budgets.'

Now, create your own 'Get-Hired' equation, which will help you to showcase succinctly your value at every interview you attend.

Stick or twist?

I've shown you one possible path. How are you feeling about it? Are you feeling optimistic or apprehensive? Or do you still feel like you want to continue rolling the dice?

If you *stick* with this choice (and it's a fine one), you will be on your way to a better job that fits more of your needs and wants. But you may want to take a look at Chapter 10 – I'm always keen to know what's behind the curtain. I'll demystify how the portfolio career works, giving you the skinny on how to make money with your gutsy ideas and market yourself without going nuts. Come on and take a peek now.

For more insights and templates on how to switch up your job role within a company or to move companies or industries, head to www.loveitleaveit.co for the Leave It Toolkit.

CHAPTER 10

CRAFTING A PORTFOLIO CAREER

What if you could wake up on Monday morning and know that you've crafted out your week to be a beautiful mix of work you care about? Work that can be done at times that suit you, with clients you adore and giving you enough spare time to see family and friends or work remotely from another country, should you wish.

It sounds intriguing and pretty exciting right? Working in a new way allows you to tap into your treasure trove of skills to create meaningful work you've always wanted to do. Equally, working in this way offers you an alternative to having to stick it out in your toxic workplace and also makes sure you don't get caught out by redundancy and economic instability by covering all your financial needs through multiple revenue streams. This beautiful blend is a Portfolio Career.

Sounds nice but what is that?

Well, it's been sexed up these days with trendy catchphrases like multi-hyphen career and side hustles. But it is fundamentally a collection of multiple strands of work (that might include part-time employment, freelancing or self-employment/owning a business) that, when combined, are equivalent to or more than one full-time job.

You may have realized that you want to work at home to be closer to your kids or perhaps you want to do three days a week in your main job and spend the rest of the week making money from your photography skills. You can create a portfolio of work that covers the mortgage and more as well as allowing you to be in control of your time.

The value of a portfolio career

There has been lots of talk about the beauty of combining many different passions and working in alternative ways to the traditional 9–5. Glamourized by the Millennial generation, I think this way of working also has a lot to offer the older individual who has spent years in a job they hate but has become risk averse due to increased responsibilities. Let's face it, when you are a young 20- or 30-something, life is much easier and your worries are lighter. As you get older, the burdens become heavier and an aversion to grand career transitions can keep you playing small.

What portfolio career do you want to create?

1. Negotiate the terms of your work or join a forward-thinking smaller, agile company + one side strand

Picture this: my former client, Angelique, worked as the PA for a large financial company. While she loved her work and it played to her strengths, something was missing for her. In the evenings, she loved tinkering with her sewing machine creating beautiful cushions for family and friends. She yearned to learn more about interior styling and design but equally knew she wasn't ready or keen to work in the industry. After all, she was happy in her role, loved her team and wasn't sure working in an interior design company would be the best financial move. With my help, she formulated a plan to approach her boss with an application to alter her working hours in order to spend one day a week experimenting in the world of interior accessories. She had an initial meeting with her boss to discuss her current role, the value she'd been providing and what her future aspirations were. After a few more meetings and a session with HR, she negotiated moving from five days down to four, giving her a day off to explore her passion. By condensing her hours, she was able to keep her pay the same and have an extra day a week to do something completely different in whatever guise she fancied, which so happened to be part-time study in interior styling.

2. Start a brand-new portfolio career with two new strands

My next client, Valentina, realized that her love for art direction, painting and yoga could work seamlessly together. Consider how the different ideas you have can end up sitting well together to create a lifestyle business with you as a freelancer or solopreneur.

Another client worked as an accountant, but always had a penchant for beautiful jewellery. Eager to differentiate herself from other accountants, she always garnered lots of compliments for her eclectic rings and necklaces. She knew there was a market for high-flying professional women who wanted to add some flair to their corporate looks. She started working with a designer and various female-owned cooperatives in Asia to manufacture the jewellery and sell them to her network. Eventually, she reduced her working days at the accountancy firm from five days to three and spent the other days concentrating on marketing, promotion and creating an e-commerce site.

Building a portfolio career allowed her to dip her toe into a new venture at low risk, grow the business organically and balance short-term accounting work. Time not working in an office is now spent travelling to source new gem stones and connect with the cooperatives she works with.

3. Use one skill or theme in a variety of ways

Perhaps you want to use your skills as a marketing consultant in a variety of ways rather than just being stuck in an office working on one brand. A mix of freelance consulting, public speaking, podcasting and online courses or training programmes could enhance your earning potential and bring in more money.

Before we get started, though, I want to get a few things straight:

- Just because you are taking your foot off the pedal with your main career doesn't mean you've given up
- This isn't an opportunity to turn your back completely on your current job. Many people I worked with or knew during my advertising and trend-innovation days were great contacts and connections that helped me make waves with my new endeavour
- I also want you to embrace a beginner's mindset. Similar to my thoughts on trialling new hobbies, there will be moments of

uncertainty, doubt, slow growth and confusion. That's all part of the journey when you leap from the certainty of working in the same place every day to try something new

This isn't a quick and easy transition. It's a fabulous choice and one I've never regretted making, but equally, it does take a bit of understanding about which routes to take.

My portfolio career roadmap

I want to showcase my roadmap and dig further into how my portfolio career has evolved over the years. Sometimes what you start out with isn't the end place but through a process of experimenting, tweaking and self-development, you can find what works for you.

Strand 1: Trend/brand consultant + Strand 2: Stylist therapist

I started with two strands that became my core revenue generators.

Stand 1: Trend consultant, absorbing all of my strengths around research and creating ideas as well as helping people see the bigger picture and the missing parts of a puzzle. I worked freelance, on temporary contracts with project-based fees and day rates, helping brands gain insight on countries they wanted to launch in.

Strand 2: Following on from my love of footwear design and fashion, I started offering a mix of online coaching and personal brand-styling packages, online e-books and in-person styling days and wardrobe diets. This blend included recurring revenue with my online coaching, e-books and large one-off payments through in-person sessions. I would plot out my months and look at how many one-day styling or wardrobe sessions I wanted to fill and the remaining days were made available for trend work.

Strand 1: Trend/brand consultant
+ Strand 2: Stylist therapist
+ Strand 3: Lecturer

Strand 3: I became a School of Life lecturer, which added another string to my bow, delivering and facilitating on average four afternoon, evening or half-day workshops per month.

Explaining my choice of career to others was met with understandable confusion but also intrigue:

- 'I thought you designed shoes... what are you doing working on trend projects?'
- 'So you teach at The School of Life, but also style women. Where do you find the time?'
- 'Which do you prefer the most? Could I do this?'

and the big one:

- 'Why don't you just focus and concentrate on one thing?'

The truth is: I didn't want to!

No two days were the same and my styling therapy work started to overtake my trend work in terms of revenue, so it became my priority.

A period of downtime and sickness meant bedrest, which allowed for learning, online training and intensive reading. I was spurred on to take courses in psychology and human behaviour.

Strand 1: Head of happiness
+ Strand 2: Stylist therapist
+ Strand 3: Lecturer

Strand 1: Keen to move completely out of trend forecasting, an opportunity to work with a company whose staff all worked from home presented itself and I grabbed it! They were trying to scale quickly, they had lots of staffing issues and no HR department. Basically, they were trying to run before they could walk. I spotted my dream opportunity and I pitched a roll-out of a new kind of people-development structure. I told them about all the transferable skills, experiences and strengths I'd amassed so far and demonstrated how they could be put to use in a way that would benefit their people. I became their Head of Happiness and from there I launched fully into the field of happiness at work. This strand has become my main bread-and-butter earner, as I consulted for two and then three days a week.

This experience opened up more opportunities to travel, live and work elsewhere. I was able to spend seven weeks over the British winter in Brazil. I moved more of my styling clients online and my lecturing was easy to plan as I had my timetable a term in advance.

Strand 1: Happiness consultant and changemaker + Strand 2: Speaker/lecturer + Strand 3: CEO of growth & happiness school

Cast your mind back to Chapter 1 where I introduced the term 'work umbrella' to encompass all the things you do. This is when I fully embraced becoming a happiness consultant, helping individuals and companies to make work happiness a priority, for example:

Strand 1: A fully fledged happiness consultant, working on long-term projects with clients and facilitating workshops, talks and running retreats – this equated to good bread-and-butter clients.

Strand 2: I become a prominent public speaker, delivering keynote speeches and conference talks and became an expert on 'happiness at work' for panels.

Strand 3: The end of 2016 to early 2017 featured horrible periods of hospitalizations and lots of time in bed. For roughly six months, I was pretty depressed and I had to decline so much work it scared me. I needed to develop passive or alternative revenue streams that didn't require me to be somewhere physically. I went back to the drawing board, creating off-the-shelf training and courses with an ambition to create a school that could produce more versions of me spreading my message out into the world. It led to my 'Be Happy First and Build A Portfolio Career' courses as well as virtual coaching and training.

The next iteration for me will include – you've guessed it, you are reading it – my first book of many to come as well as a move towards more product-based and tech offerings, and growing my teams of international happiness consultants. As I enter a new life phase, leveraging a business beyond me is my focus.

As always, I want to be realistic. I don't want to leave you feeling as if this was a quick and easy transition. I've never regretted making the leap, but equally it does take hard work and some understanding about which routes to take.

On my journey helping people convert their skills into a portfolio career, I've noticed a pattern of initial questions:

- 'I've been (insert your profession here) for my entire career and don't know what else I can do'
- 'I've recently left my full-time job to start a portfolio career, I didn't really have a structured plan and now I catch myself looking at jobs I don't want because I can't make it work'
- 'I'm a product development manager with a love for organization psychology. Do you think I can do both?'
- 'I have lots of great ideas – new ones every week – where do I put my energy first?'
- 'I'm already doing this, but struggling to manage two careers. How do I balance my time, energy and headspace?'
- 'I make jewellery as well as work part-time as an accountant. I have trouble talking about what I do as both audiences are so different. What do I say when someone asks me what I do?'

Over the years I've started to map out the stages that someone goes through when they're stuck when considering or working in a portfolio career.

The ten cycles of portfolio career frustration

1. Motivation: 'YES A PORTFOLIO CAREER IS FOR ME! I'm excited to make this work. I can do this!'
2. Convincer mode: 'It's going to be OK, everyone, I'm finally going to be happy in my work.'
3. Analysis paralysis: 'So, from my five ideas, I'm going with this one first... or maybe this one... or perhaps this one because...'
4. Reality setting in: 'Ugh, this is trickier than I thought. Why can't I make this work?'
5. Remotivation: 'OK, I just went to this amazing talk/read this blog... I've got it all sorted out now.'
6. Judgement: 'Oh god, they are going to ask me what I do. I don't know what to say. It was so much easier to say I was [insert job] before.'
7. Embarrassment: 'Eek, I'm short again this month. I can't seem to work out the right mix of activities to make the money I need.'
8. Overwhelm: 'I've said yes to every client. Now I've got way too much on my plate, more than I can manage.'
9. Exhaustion: 'I thought I'd be sitting at home in my pjs. Why am I so tired and stressed all the time?'
10. Resignation: 'I'm never going to be able to do this.'

I'm going to be honest with you. Getting stuck and frustrated happens to everyone, including smart people and successful people. Our inner critic can hold us back from pushing full steam ahead with any changes we want to make. This happens to **everyone**! The key is to identify why and where you are stuck exactly. Luckily, I've got some exercises to help you unravel this and start off your portfolio career successfully.

How to cut through the frustration: you are stuck in the 'ideas haze'

Consider the following: No passions/strengths/ideas versus too many passions/strengths/ideas. Two very different problems, but the result is the same – analysis paralysis. Many of us are obsessed with the search for the right ideas that we can't settle on what to start with. Then we tend to say self-defeating things such as, 'Can I really balance two opposing skills/ passions?' or 'I may as well just stay where I am.'

The truth is it's about creating a combination of portfolio strands that are PROFITABLE and FEEL RIGHT and taking it from there.

But what do I mean by 'portfolio strands'? Think of knitting yarn or a piece of rope – long, continuous interlocked fibres used to produce textiles. You need to think of your portfolio career as weaving together individual 'strands' to make one cohesive career. This means thinking about how these individual 'strands' will provide money and how much time they will take up in your working week. Rather than the one job 'strand' you are currently used to, you need to think about creating multiple strands, each with its own earning potential.

Here are just a few combinations I've helped my clients with:

- Sticking with your bread-and-butter job + revving up your passion project? Accountancy and Jewellery.
- Or do you want to follow in Leonardo da Vinci's footsteps as a left brain + right brain doer? Coder and Painter and Carpenter.
- Do you want to balance the physical + mental in your work? Yoga Therapist + Painter + Art Director.
- Have a common thread that works across any field? Like me, happiness at work – Author/Facilitator/Speaker/Podcaster/ Consultant/Coach.

More often than not, people will spend hours and hours combing through lists of passions, ideas and directions as if the 'right one' will magically jump out at them rather than focusing on the right combination of strands for them.

In this section, we will be working through five exercises to help you nail down your ideas once and for all!

EXERCISE

The five Ws

WHO Identify your ideal clients, role models, customers, colleagues.

WHERE What location or which industry or companies do you want to join/replicate?

WAY What do you want your portfolio career to look like?

WHAT Which skills, strengths are you using?

WHY What are your values? What's driving you to do this?

The 5 Ws	Portfolio career idea – example 1	Portfolio career idea – example 2	It's your turn...
	I've got a passion for food and I'm a mum who wants to feed my kids nutritious meals on a budget. I don't want to work full time in my current job as a social-media manager.	I love being an accountant but I find my work uninspiring. I'm earning well, working in a contract position, and I want to use my skills for social good.	
Who	I want to work with mums who want to create healthy meals for their newborns and young toddlers.	I love the energy and innovation in start-ups. Maybe I could investigate providing my skills in accountancy at start-up hubs while still working in my main job.	
Where	I want to mainly sell products online so I can be at home with my kids.	I love living in London but would be open to travelling to do this.	
Way	Combining my existing job as a social media manager and creating online recipe plans and courses.	Renegotiating my working week so that I can do this maybe one day a week and evenings.	
What	Design, Tech, People skills.	Providing accountancy services to young entrepreneurs at a local co-working space or start-up hub.	
Why	Freedom – I want to travel and choose my own hours.	I value using my skills to elevate others to make better decisions.	

EXERCISE

Stress test that strand – Part 1

In this second exercise, I want you to stress test each strand to see if it's going to provide you with the necessary money you need to fund the rest of your life and be a viable option.

This will help you to extract all the potential possibilities, so that you don't feel like a headless chicken trying to make your portfolio career work. There are six fault lines where your portfolio career can start to crack, so let's take a look at what they are:

1. Market opportunity: How viable is what you want to create/do/become? Are there many people doing it? Is the market mature, saturated or at an early stage? What could be your USP? If you are moving into this field as a consultant, do you know how much you can command?

2. Fun score: You don't get into this to be bored as f**k so will this work bring you joy? I think a lot of people get into certain types of work because they think the job will be lucrative. The reality is that you must have a passion to push through and show up before the mega bucks start flowing otherwise, my friend, you will come unstuck.

3. Connections in the field: How can you leverage your existing network to help you? If you don't know anyone doing this work, how will you start to find them?

4. Toolkit alignment: Think back to Chapter 5 and your strengths and skills toolkit (see page 60). There is no point building a portfolio career that doesn't play to this otherwise you will be working against your natural talents. Obviously, there will be a few areas that you may need to get help with, for example, if accounting isn't your bag and you need to write a business plan for investment in your new pop-up coffee shop, you might need to get some help.

5. Potential revenue options: How will you choose to make your money? Do you need a set amount of recurring monthly cash? Or could you be OK with larger, project-based work that takes up perhaps six months of your time, but leaves you with six months to devote to your other work strand? We will be covering this in more detail shortly.

6. Ease of entry: How quickly can you get your portfolio career up and running, i.e. start working in a new area, integrate it into your week and begin to earn money from it? What other barriers might you come up against? For example, if you want to create software, have you got the upfront investment to work with developers before it gains traction?

Take a look at the example from the previous exercise:
I've got a passion for food and I'm a mum who wants to feed my kids nutritious meals on a budget. I don't want to work full time in my current job as a social media manager. I'd like to find a way to combine my passion for cooking nutritious foods for children with social media marketing.

STRAND 1: Meal planning and recipe ideas for new mums, involving online recipes, supermarket shopping shortcuts and blogs and videos.

STRAND 2: Social media management job.

Look at the table on the following pages, then have a go at filling in your own examples.

Portfolio strand	Market opportunity	Fun score	Connections in this field
1 Meal planning and recipe ideas for new mums	Big. I've been looking at online forums and it's a huge issue. Plus I've just become a new mum and I share these pains alongside the other new mums I meet. I can make my offering more unique by catering to various intolerances which my baby has, so I'm super-knowledgeable.	I love food. I'm always thinking of new recipes that save time. I like meeting new people.	I don't know anyone else doing this
2 Social media manager	I'm in a company that's growing and my work can be done virtually. I have a good rapport with my boss so will propose a part-time working arrangement.	My company is exciting and the work is always different. I'm never bored.	Lots! I've spent years working in this field. I already know some people who could help me spread the word for my meal-planning business.
It's your turn... **1**			
2			

Toolkit alignment	Potential revenue options	Ease of entry
I'm creative. I love connecting with people. I can use social media platforms so I can promote myself. I might need to learn more about money management and pricing.	Online recipe guides – good passive revenue (see passive revenue, page 188) Supermarket shopping – could be a monthly subscription idea to do the shopping.	I just need: • my laptop • a camera to take good photos • money for website and marketing
I have access to all the latest tools and insights on social-media marketing so I'm constantly growing here.	Bread-and-butter monthly salary which covers most of our family outgoings. Plus I'm still eligible for some of my bonuses even when part-time.	I'm already doing it!

EXERCISE

Stress test that strand – Part 2

Research business models

What if your portfolio career consists of your day job, plus a brand-new business you are keen to set up with a friend perhaps? A portfolio career is the perfect way to test your business idea and shape the business pitch while still working part-time or short-term contract hours until you are ready to make the leap.

Which business model is right for you?

Pick some businesses that are relevant to the line of work you want to move into and ask yourself the following questions:

- How would you conduct an existing business differently?
- What are the key frustrations you've experienced as a user of a product/service in an existing business model that you are keen to explore?
- How will your idea upgrade a current product/service or innovate entirely?
- How could you borrow an idea and refine the concept, find companies to partner with or franchise/licence in order to shortcut your business journey?

Once you've established the model, what prototype can you create for your service and product?

- Is it a new organic beauty line specifically for BAME Gen Z individuals looking for an affordable price point and a community element? *A further play on Glossier perhaps?*
- Is it a clothing subscription service for entrepreneurial and professional men aged between 35–50 years who hate shopping but want to look stylish? *Mr Porter meets Netflix?*
- Is it a wellness app for not-for-profit companies keen to support their frontline staff with mental and physical wellbeing? *Headspace for the charity sector?*

You may have noticed the detail I have given for each of these target markets and product/service offerings. I'm hoping that you can get this detailed too.

EXERCISE

Stress test that strand – Part 3

Keep testing your idea

It's important to understand what exactly you are good at, what comes naturally to you and how you want to use this passion/skill/idea from your toolkit from Chapter 5 (see page 60). Then you need to test your idea to see if it really works and whether it is aligned to your values and your life goals as well as being profitable.

You can start to test your idea by implementing the minimal viable product (MVP) process. This is essentially a product or service that you create with basic or minimal features that is enough to get the attention of your first set of customers. You want to produce a stripped-down or paired-back version of your end product that is enough to be attention-grabbing and provide a response from prospective buyers. This initial feedback will then go some way to helping you refine and distil the product down to the final offering, minus all the weaknesses.

If we take the example earlier (see page 179), you could gather together a small focus group of new mums and do some research on what their pain points are and what they would be prepared to pay for. Then create a selection of five basic menu cards at a lower price than you would want to charge, get them to test some of the recipes over a two-week period and ask for feedback. Once you've made the tweaks, you can rejig your offering and gradually increase your prices once you have a product/service that is in demand. These early-stage testers can provide you with necessary testimonials for your new website, which always helps with future sales.

EXERCISE

Dissect your idea

At this point, many people get distracted by spending too much time perfecting their website or printing snazzy business cards before even checking if the idea is profitable or how to make it so. Then they venture off with a random set of thoughts or ideas, not really knowing exactly how to move it all into action. Using the previous exercises and doing your research, I want you to be able to confidently answer the following sentences:

- My first idea (the original light-bulb idea you came up with) is...
- The type of audience I'm drawn to is (your target market)...
- I know this audience has the ability to pay because (what tells you they can afford what you are offering)...
- My solution helps to remedy the... (pain points of your audience)...

  by... (explain how you will help)...
- After researching, testing and talking to potential customers, I believe my end idea (the next phase of the idea, after learning more about target market, costs to market) is...
- What I learned through this process about my service/product and my potential attitude to make this work is...

Now you should have concrete insights on what will work and what ideas you may need to tweak or forget about altogether. Set yourself a time limit on how long you will spend researching and testing your MVP before leaping into it completely – will it be one week, two or six months of research and testing? It will depend on what your product/service is as well as the time and resources you have available. Ultimately, I want you to get started versus procrastinating, so be realistic and rigid with your timeline and get some friends or family to hold you accountable to it too.

How to cut through the frustration: providing the income you need

If you work twice as hard at a regular job, you still make the SAME income; you may get the odd bonus here and there, but ultimately you are stuck with your salary. With a portfolio career, once you've experimented and tested different strands, you can work twice as hard and double or triple your potential income.

Scale up as much – or as little – as you want. With the right 'Portfolio Pie Mix' (see below) in place, you can work in a way that suits the available time you have and helps you balance the risk.

Portfolio pie mix

I created this framework to help clients keep track of what role each portfolio strand plays in their pie and what revenue they can hope to achieve from each. Below are the different levels – bear in mind that you can manipulate these to suit you, but the amount you have the potential to earn decreases as you go down the list.

Star work

This is essentially a piece of work that you can charge a bigger cash lump sum for, delivered in a shorter amount of time. An example of this is my public speaking work. These vary from a 30-minute keynote talk to an after-dinner speech and Q&A session or one-day strategy session. I'm particular about how many pieces of star work I do per quarter because, while it looks like just a short time on stage or is just a one-day session, it does require a lot of behind-the-scenes prep with the client, rehearsing the speech and so on.

Bread and butter

A continuous flow of money that comes in monthly or on a regular basis for a set period of time. For example, paid employment, contract work, coaching. In my case, these are one-to-one coaching clients that run on a three-month programme or corporate retainers which are between six and twelve months long.

Learning opportunity

An environment that allows you to test (new) products or content on a new audience, flex your muscles learning new skills or more about your target market's pain points and concerns. For me, these are my School of Life workshops that I do once a month or masterclasses using my own content that I deliver at the *Guardian*.

Semi/passive revenue

This is typically a project where you put the hard graft in upfront, which then generates income without day-to-day involvement. For example, royalties from books, e-products/courses/training, licences/patents, software/apps and music. So my book, *Love It or Leave It*, is in this section.

Freebies

This is activity that allows your audience to learn about your brand, your services and products. For example, your monthly newsletters, social media shares and posts or blog articles that offer valuable information. It could also be talks at large conferences or events that expose you to an untapped, wider audience and help you build contacts and brand awareness. Freebies can also be free discovery calls you offer to help someone learn more about your service. Examples from my end include my monthly newsletter, free podcasts, my free happiness consult calls and talks events in London or conventions abroad.

Portfolio pie mix examples

Accountancy + Jewellery designer:

Star work

- Jewellery commissions

Bread and butter

- Accountancy – short- to long-term contracts
- Freelance accountant for hubs that support start-up businesses

Learning opportunity

- Trade show events – talks, trunk shows and stalls for the jewellery

Passive revenue

- Sales of jewellery online

Creative art director + Artist/painter + Yoga teacher:

Star work

- Advertising stints with creative partner – blocks of 3–6 months of good pay

Bread and butter

- Yoga – group sessions every Sunday at different venues in London
- Yoga – working with a team of yoga teachers, arranging sessions in various university campuses across the UK

Learning opportunity

- Art roadshows, open-house sessions and pop-up craft markets – ad hoc and seasonal

Passive revenue

- Art sales

Podcaster + Speaker + SAAS (software as a service):

Star work

- Speaking at conferences – seasonal

Bread and butter/passive revenue

- Affiliate marketing – recommending books, podcasts, software tools and other people's courses, making a fee on every item sold
- Podcasting sponsorship – fee paid monthly or quarterly or annually
- Podcasting software – recurring software subscription to help you create and launch your own podcast and hosting them
- Two books – passive royalty revenues
- Online courses – ongoing enrollment
- Semi-passive – office hour calls once a month

Freebies

- Online blog
- Facebook Live events
- YouTube channel – live Q&As
- Instagram Stories

How to cut through the frustration: you struggle to market yourself and your portfolio career

For some people, the constant need to explain what you do and what you have to offer takes its toll. Whether you are attending a networking party, a dinner or a wedding celebration, there is one dreaded question that has most budding portfolio careerists quaking in their shoes: 'So, what do you do?'

So much of our identity is wrapped up in our work. Work informs our goals, shapes our personalities and sends a message about our values. Often the company you work in allows you to step into a cloak of desirability, aspiration and prowess around its brand.

When we leave a company, it can be hard to know what we stand for or if we can make ourselves heard in a new landscape. It's important that we do because if we don't, good luck trying to get work.

I've had clients tell me that when they describe their portfolio career, some people assume they are a generalist. The challenge of marketing ourselves to different audiences about what we do can raise stress levels. We have to take into consideration how we present ourselves. It is easier to present yourself as a super-multifaceted creative on The Dots (a creative networking site), but if you are an IT specialist at a corporate bank and a personal trainer, curating this on social media and LinkedIn isn't easy.

Creating a one-line description of what you do – your 'work umbrella' – helps define who you are and invites listeners to get curious about what you do. Then it's up to you to dive into what's relevant to your audience. It gives you the flexibility to play up or down what you do according to the situation and the audience – the world we live in is opening up so much.

So how do you create a portfolio work umbrella? For mine, I use 'helping people be happy first' or 'making work happiness a priority'. Here are some other examples:

- 'Teller of visual stories' (photographer and textile designer)
- 'I offer accounting services with a side of style' (accountancy and jewellery designer)

Create your own work umbrella by following the exercise overleaf.

EXERCISE

Create your work umbrella

In this exercise, craft a title or one-line description of yourself that defines who you are and offers an insight into what you can do. Below are a few points to think about:

- Think of at least one idea for your audience to remember.
- Who are you really? Who are you beyond your title? People buy people so it's important to show why you care about what you do and let that come across in your personality, your dress, your mannerisms and attitude. In my case, I'm passionate about this work as it's been a journey of my own discovery to find work happiness. I'm also eccentric, approachable, calming and fun, and it comes across in how I dress, my business branding and my interactions with people.
- Why should your audience care? You have to convey the reasons why people should listen to you. We are in a very noisy world and your work has to resonate with your target client immediately, so you need to find ways to address their pain points and how you can help them.
- What's in it for them? This is essentially the help that clients can expect to receive from you. When they exchange their time and money, what can they expect to get in return?
- What is your authentic look and feel?

How to cut through the frustration: how to balance mind and body with work

Last but not least, it's important to make sure the wheels don't fall off! Have you ever noticed that some days you have all the time in the world, but you still can't get anything done?

It's not just about TIME – it's also about ENERGY and MOTIVATION.

'I don't deal well with uncertainty.' Most stress comes from not knowing where money or work is coming from. But once you learn how to design each of your portfolio strands and master your money, you will start to create a clear and viable path to manage the risk and minimize this anxiety.

'My mood is so up and down.' Sometimes you are full of glee, working on a new project or talking with potential customers and then other times, it seems easier to just pull the duvet covers over and go back to sleep.

When sh*t hits the fan, how do you find that internal anchor to stay on track? What will you focus on when the going gets tough? Knowing how to talk about your business, your successes, your losses and your mindset is key.

Manifestos that past clients have used include:

- 'I will make sure that I'm well fed and watered daily, so I can be at my best'
- 'I will make sure that I look at my business numbers regularly and not shy away from them'
- 'I will surround myself with good people, resources and energy'
- 'I will be mindful about the workload and clients I take on so that I can deliver great work'
- 'I will talk about my business with positivity rather than dwell on losses'

We will be diving deeper into how you can maintain your personal happiness later on. But first let's simply look at how you can start to map out your week.

EXERCISE

Visualize your ideal working week

It's important to manage your energy and time when building a portfolio career. Whether you have fixed employment days and two days working on your own thing or the freedom to plan out your week entirely, I always recommend that your weeks need to include chunks of time for the following:

Admin

As the name suggests, it's the grease that keeps your work and life turning:

Life admin

- Checking in on your self-care
- Health appointments, nail care, haircuts, assessing your monthly expenses and setting budgets
- Groceries

Working on the business

- Assessing the sales and costs in the business
- Invoicing
- Catching up with your team

Basically, this is all about optimizing and sustaining any structure that enables your life and business to function.

Delivery

This is the actual 'work' that makes up your portfolio career. Here are some examples to get you started:

- Working on my happiness consultancy business on Tuesday to Thursday with workshops, teaching, consulting and coaching
- Flying every other month as an air stewardess and using my months not working to build my styling empire
- Selling pottery creations at the market on Friday to Sunday and spending Tuesday and Wednesday as a receptionist

Blue-sky thinking

This is when you aren't just chasing your tail thinking about what you are doing next week, but actively giving yourself time to think about the future and the exciting possibilities.

- ➤ Visualizing and strategizing
- ➤ Making vision boards
- ➤ Getting perspective. Asking what do I want?
- ➤ Checking in with your manager about your goals, future pay-rise opportunities or personal development ideas
- ➤ Taking time to get to know the people you work with

Creative time

The time spent getting those creative juices flowing to develop yourself and/ or your portfolio career.

- ➤ Experimentation and perhaps working on some of your action steps from the Ideas Lab exercise in Chapter 8 (see page 141)
- ➤ Writing creative PR and marketing features for your business
- ➤ New blogs or recording an interview for your new podcast show

Rejuvenation

Everyone needs to replenish and recharge.

- ➤ Time with friends, time for yourself, meeting people, space for creativity
- ➤ Yoga, meditation, gym
- ➤ Journalling or recording your thoughts on your phone

By making sure you have time for each of these areas over your working week you will keep the wheels of your portfolio career turning nicely. Each week I map out what my working week looks like and how I can plan for incoming work. What would your dream working week look like?

I'm out the door

So that's your tour of Leave It options! How do you feel?

I know it's a lot to take in, but pace yourself, investigate and decide what feels right for you. What you decide on now isn't set in stone. You might move from one option to another and that's OK. You may leave to find another job and then meet a potential business partner you could start a new venture with. Alternatively, you may find that once you negotiate your work terms, you have the space to create a portfolio career. Like I said, career transitions are ever-evolving, so strap up, and be open to chance and opportunity.

It's easy to get high with bright ideas and then flounder again a few days later. Keeping the momentum going is key to successfully completing any change. In the next section, we will look at this as well as getting your finances in shape, helping you build the community to support you and waving goodbye to work situations that no longer suit you with gratitude and grace.

Stick with me. The adventure isn't over yet.

Visit www.loveitleaveit.co for additional resources, tools, templates and book recommendations for this chapter.

SECTION 6:
YOU'VE GOT THIS!

CHAPTER 11

KEEPING THE MOMENTUM

So far in this book, the action has been confined to your head. You've been ruminating and reflecting. Now, I'd like to move you outwards, from internal reflection to the realities of your surroundings, your circumstances and the relationships you have or need to seek.

Let's not lie to ourselves, amid all the excitement about treading a new path you probably have some murmurings of worry, questioning and panic:

- How will I actually make all this work financially?
- How will my partner react if I decide to change roles and it affects my pay?
- I'm scared to leave my colleagues, but I know I'm not happy – saying goodbye is going to be hard

Rome wasn't built in a day and, like any transition, it can feel like four steps forward and two steps back. The fact is, I know you've got this! You've come this far, so I know you are made of strong stuff. I just want to make sure you look at a few last areas to help you keep momentum and make it to your end goal, whatever that may turn out to be.

We'll be addressing several key areas:

- The thorny issue of money and whether or not you can afford to leave your current job
- How to build your support system
- How to deal with failure
- How to see the bright side of moving on

Can you afford to leave it?

Money is always a tricky topic, but we've got to address the elephant in the room. Most of the time when I deliver workshops, money is one of the significant reasons people stay in jobs they don't love or feel paralysed about making changes.

I live in one of the most expensive cities in the world: London. That may or may not be the same for you, but the reality is that money is necessary to keep a roof over my head and food in the fridge among other things. I'm guessing it's the same for you, whether you want to:

- Drop from five days a week to three to build a portfolio career.
- Encourage and support your partner's shift in departments which comes with a slight pay decrease
- Take six months off on a sabbatical to explore your options
- Launch your business in the next nine months
- Build a community for your new product before you launch it
- Create prototypes for a new business

These decisions all require you to have some solid foundations in place. We've become too used to instant gratification. At the click of a button, we can order cabs, books, meals, you name it, and they arrive the same day. But while we might want work happiness to come quickly and immediately, the biggest barrier to this happening is often money, or lack of it.

I never encourage my clients to quit on a whim. Unless you are working in an incredibly toxic environment, quitting your job, while radical and self-affirming, can send you into a dark and miserable place. It's hard to be in a place of creativity and growth when you are constantly worrying about a lack of resources. It pays to have some level of awareness of what you are working with, what you need, where you can take calculated risks and where you need to trim the excess.

Month in and month out

What's the amount you need each month to cover all your outgoings? Do you know? If not, why not?

When I ask my clients this, not everyone can give a complete figure on the spot. It's important that we get money literate if we want to win at work happiness. It will empower you to know what steps you can make confidently and where the stretch is too much.

I wasn't always money savvy. When I think back to the days of making shoes, I definitely overstretched myself across credit cards, burned through bonuses at work and perhaps should have built several assets a lot earlier. I was naive, scared to look at the numbers and basically digging my head into the sand. When I started to do more one-to-one personal branding and style therapy work, I was elated at the revenue coming in and, again, I didn't always divert it into places most people (my parents) would have wanted. I chose to upskill, retrain and travel. All life- and work-happiness-enhancing, but had I portioned up my money more effectively, I could have pushed further in other areas like buying a house which I could have rented out when I spent time abroad instead of continuing to pay rent. You live and you learn. I decided to increase my financial literacy to create the stronger base I work from today. For me, there was always that worry in my head that my health issues had a tendency to scupper my earning capacity. Paying attention to building up my assets, creating multiple revenue streams and knowing my worth became a way of life to me and helped me sleep easier at night.

By carefully managing your income, you can make sure that you cover all your bases and reach your goals. I learned the concept of dividing my monthly income from Ann Wilson, The Wealth Chef and international finance coach, whose mission it is to empower men and women to have more financial literacy. She suggests dividing your monthly income into portions, and any money left over can be spent on other areas. I decided to divide my portions into savings jars in a way that resonated with me.

Jar 1: Everyday items = 55 per cent. This is your mortgage or rent, bills, food and clothes. Being careful with your spending here will help you add more to your 'Big-ticket items' and 'Brain food' jars.

Jar 2: Good times = 10 per cent because life's too short to be serious all the time. Even in the midst of being mindful with your spending and saving, all work and no play makes Sammy very dull. I like to use this jar for whimsical adventures, treats (you know I love my shoes) and foodie experiences.

Jar 3: Long-term, rainy day savings = 10 per cent of your money that you can put directly into asset building, such as buying stocks and shares. This should only be touched in an emergency.

Jar 4: Big-ticket items = 10 per cent for saving now if you are thinking of quitting your job later. This nest egg should be your safety net. Most people use this for holidays, property or children's education, but I advise clients in the 'Love It or Leave It' quandary to start looking at this as their jar to keep them afloat if they decide to quit suddenly or as a buffer between starting a business/portfolio career and it becoming profitable.

Jar 5: Charity donations = 5 per cent because it's always important to give back. Even if 5 per cent feels too much, do what you can. Helping others enhances our wellbeing, too.

Jar 6: Brain food = 10 per cent to invest in yourself. Education, training, books, networking events, conferences and summits. If you save in this way, you will have enough for the odd course or networking event. For more expensive courses, you can use your 'Big-ticket items' jar, too. Knowledge is power and, if you know that your next move in or outside of work requires learning, make the space and invest.

Side note: If you are self-employed or a business owner, you will need to make provision for your taxes. For those of you who are thinking about starting a business or already running one and want to create an automated system for your personal and business finances you should read the brilliant book *Profit First* by Mike Michalowicz (see page 269).

Most banking apps will allow you to create 'jars' or separate accounts for you to apportion the money accordingly and help you stick to a budget.

I like to automate Jars 3 and 4 with direct debits into savings accounts so that I don't miss the money. When you are going through a period of experimenting, it will help you to know that you have money building up for when you are ready to leap.

Try the exercise on the next page to help you get a sense of how you can best use the money you have.

EXERCISE

Working out your money

This is an exercise for you to look at what's coming in, what's going out, and where you can grow your savings and development jars faster so that you can move on with ease and less stress.

Step one

To create good money habits, we have to see exactly what we are spending month to month. I would advise you to do this for the last twelve months but, for illustrative purposes, I have shown you how to get started with three months. Use your last three months' bank statements to analyse where your hard-earned cash money is going. It's important that you get to grips with:

- The money that comes into your life – salary, paid client work, product sales
- The money that flows out of your life – credit card debits, loans, student debt, treats, holidays, housing costs, bills, subsistence, travel, car, etc

Outgoings	Month 1	Month 2	Month 3
Everyday expenses			
Utilities			
Loan payment			
Mortgage or rent			
Council tax			
Food shopping			
Insurance			
Good-times expenses			
Shoes			
Cinema trips			

Outgoings	Month 1	Month 2	Month 3
Nights out			
Takeaways or restaurant dinners			
Long-term savings			
ISA monthly direct debit			
Stocks – regular investment			
Charity			
Monthly direct debit to charity			
Brain food			
Networking events			
Evening writing course			
TOTAL			

Step two

Now it's time to set some boundaries and portion out your monthly money so that you can see what's possible to save, put towards education or training and what you can save to splurge on a holiday.

You can start to play around with the levels of income you are making and what difference they will make to your life and living once you start to earn more or less.

- Lowest basic: What is the absolute basic you can live on (i.e. no frills)?
- Happy medium: What's the next level up that allows you to maintain the kind of lifestyle you are accustomed to?
- Dream: This is where you get to live and work according to your dream lifestyle without restrictions or hesitation.

Continued overleaf

MONEY IN	JAR 1 55 per cent	JAR 2 10 per cent	JAR 3 10 per cent	JAR 4 10 per cent	JAR 5 5 per cent	JAR 6 10 per cent
LOWEST BASIC 2,500 per month	1,375	250	250	250	125	250
HAPPY MEDIUM 6,000 per month	3,000	600	600	600	600	300
DREAM 20,000 per month	11,000	2,000	2,000	2,000	1,000	2,000

Step three

If you are deciding to leave your job, take a pay cut or start a business or portfolio career, you may need to rejig your budget to make sure you and your household can still function.

Perhaps you've given yourself a 6–9-month deadline before you quit your job. As your current income comes in, you might decide to increase or decrease your percentage splits to help you save more, pour more money into training or education or curb your good times jar for a while.

Money in	Current percentage	Changed percentage to	Keep the same
Jar 1 Everyday items	55	50	
Jar 2 Good times	10	5	
Jar 3 Long-term savings	10	0	
Jar 4 Big-ticket items	10	25	
Jar 5 Charity donations	5		5
Jar 6 Brain food	10	15	

Giving yourself some financial breathing space

You may fall into one of two camps:

1. You are thinking about setting up your accounts like the example above, so that you have a base to start building from.
2. You already have that in place and now you need to assess how long your savings and other assets can support you if you don't earn an income for a while.

Where do you go from here? Tackling the following questions will help you ascertain some critical points in your plan that need your attention.

- What would happen after 6–9 months of not working or bringing in enough income to meet your day-to-day living expenses? If you have stocks, what could you sell?
- How much do you have in savings? How long would you last if you just lived off your savings?

What are your assets and liabilities?

- Your assets might include:

  Equity: ISAs, stocks and shares, bonds and mutual funds. In essence, they are your share in the profits of somebody else's business.

  Income-generating property: residential or commercial, but not your private home. Properties where you receive income in the form of rent.

  Semi-passive and passive income businesses: for example, royalties from books, e-products, courses, training, patents, software, apps and music.
- If you're working towards your first house or rental venture, keep at it! You can still build assets on a budget by investing in shares for very small amounts per month or using 'round up' apps or 'jars' in your bank accounts. So, if you spend £2.75 on your daily coffee, it will round it up to £3.00 and save 25p to a stocks and shares ISA. Building your assets one penny at a time!

- Your liabilities. What do you owe? Consumer credit cards, loans, student debt

These calculations may feel more pertinent for those starting businesses or opting for a portfolio career because of the concern if either of these options takes longer to make money than you projected.

Equally, you could move to another job and suddenly find yourself in a pickle if the company hits a bad patch and has to lay off people. It could be a case of 'last in, first out'. How long could you survive? Being an active participant in your work happiness means preparing for every money eventuality.

What if I need more money?

If you find you need to top up your money reserves, it's time to think about what opportunities you have available to make this happen.
I want to refresh your memory with some of the different revenue models in Chapter 10 (see pages 187–8). As you read through them, grab a notebook and note which model is the best way for you to generate more income:

Star work
This is a direct match of skills and talents and often takes up a smaller amount of time for a bigger cash gain. In some cases, however, these big-ticket jobs may or may not be as frequent as bread-and-butter options.

Bread and butter
This is a continuous flow of steady money that comes in monthly or after a set period of time – paid employment, contract work, coaching or therapy sessions.

Semi/passive revenue
This includes royalties and revenues from books, software, apps and music.

Bridging loans

These are often used to 'bridge the gap' between selling a property and buying another, but they can be used for more or less any business purpose. Perhaps you want to make a first-time property investment at an auction. Or maybe you're looking to refurbish a property to increase the yield. It doesn't even have to be related to property either. You can use it for any short-term capital injection, for example, if you don't have the upfront cash to pay your corporation tax.

Side hustle

Otherwise known as 'side gigs'. What is the marketable skill, service or product you can offer that will bring in a bit of extra cash when you are still working full time and want to top up your 'Big-ticket items' or 'Brain food' jars? These side hustles should tap into a market that can afford to pay, feel like fun to you and, in some cases, leverage or build your skills or help you meet new contacts or connections.

EXERCISE

Topping up the money box

What is your financial status at the moment? If you want to increase your long-term savings and brain food pots, you have to make more money. It might come from negotiating a pay rise or if you have a business or portfolio career, you may need to look at various ways to up your income level.

For this exercise, read through the various revenue streams on the previous pages, grab a notebook and note down which model is the best way for you to generate some more income. Then take a moment to reflect on the questions below and complete the boxes to find ways to top up your money box.

Current monthly income or revenue	How much more would I like to earn?	Where could this come from?	By when?
5,000	1,000	Teaching kids computer programs two evenings a week. Pay rise. Listing my flat on AirBnB when I am away.	Within the next six months.

Trimming your spending to help you move forwards

We don't all have a saver mentality. But if you or your partner are thinking of making drastic changes in your work life, it pays to be mindful of your money outflows and especially where you can turn off a few leaky taps. I'm not saying you've got to live on beans on toast, but how can you maintain some level of normality without all the dead weight that perhaps isn't necessary to your life?

Here are a few ways to shed some unwanted expenses to make way for a brighter future:

- Bank fees – most people don't have a clue what fees they are paying. What are yours and how can you change to a low-cost or no-fee account?
- Interest payments – are you paying just the minimum every month on your cards or loans? Can you overpay to starve the interest monster?
- Insurances – it's one of those things you question and when you don't have it, boy do you feel it, but can you make tweaks to your life, home, car and medical insurance to save some money?
- Utilities – proactively compare offers and switch to get better rates
- Food, glorious food – do you buy a lot of prepackaged and ready-made food? Do you have a takeaway habit? Stop it! Try cooking double the quantity and freezing the extra amount to take to work for lunch
- Buy your grocery shopping monthly online with prepared lists – this changed the game for me. Now I meal prep in advance as much as I can to limit waste. Equally, there's nothing wrong with buying your household items from bulk wholesalers
- Subscriptions and memberships – if you use the gym, fantastic, but the reality for some is that after the January buzz, gyms become graveyards and just scoop up your payment every month without a word of thanks. Could you cancel your membership? How often are you using all those apps, magazine and course subscriptions? Could you cancel any?
- Make your own skin, hair, beauty and cleaning products, then at least you know what is in them and you can reduce your exposure to toxic chemicals

- Detox your wardrobe and house and sell any unwanted items causing clutter
- Once a month, have a no-money day. This is a fun day where you come up with an idea to have a day out without spending any money.
- Track your spending by using budgeting apps or spreadsheets like You Need A Budget (www.youneedabudget.com)

What else could you do to meet your bigger work-happiness goals?

Your work-happiness support system

What if, in the quest to live life with purpose and follow your mission, you falter, get tripped up or just grow tired? That's inevitable, my friend! I can't and won't sugarcoat it. When we choose 'courage over comfort', as Brené Brown would say, we step into a place of unknowing but it will be worth it to achieve the new growth you desire.

When it comes to picking a new route and keeping steadfast on the journey it's important to embrace my BE HAPPY FIRST roadmap.

Your first reaction might be unease: 'Who am I to put myself first? It feels selfish.' This isn't a selfish manifesto at all. It's one born out of love and compassion to ensure that whatever impact you want to have in the world, whatever change you want to create, you can do it without compromising the precious commodity you have – yourself.

All too often, we can get carried away trying to create impact/ideas/money/change/wellness/happiness (delete as appropriate) for our customers, co-workers, teams or families and friends and end up burning ourselves out.

There are 7 elements of the BE HAPPY FIRST model:

Be kind, aware, present

Increase awareness of your triggers, identify where to invest your energy and initiate the right habits for greater success and wellness, adopting signature mindfulness and happiness techniques to stay grounded. Check back to Chapter 4 to look at core self-care steps to overcome stress and Chapter 7 for the Body scan exercise (see page 134).

Expose

Learn how to embrace vulnerability (at work), how to ask for help successfully to get yourself to the next level and supercharge the success you desire. We discussed where to get help if you are feeling overwhelmed about your career at the end of Chapter 4 (see pages 48–54).

Hang up

Identify which personal 'hang-ups' to let go of that are standing in your way of success. What do you need to let go of, put down, make peace with to make the changes you desire? Later on, we will look at how to let go of work that no longer suits you and how to ask for support.

Appreciate

Find ways to show appreciation for others, and opportunities on your work-happiness path, and acknowledge the challenges and obstacles, as well as yourself, in a way that's conscious and meaningful. Refer back to 'Remind yourself that you are awesome' (see Chapter 5, pages 59–79) to remind yourself what amazing skills and strengths you've gathered in your life that will help you in your next move.

Pick up

When it comes to getting the best out of your work (and life), is it all going according to plan? It's not enough to know what your strengths are. You need to be able to apply them intelligently and challenge yourself to pick up new ones. Challenge yourself frequently to try new things and have a beginner's mind attitude. If you need a recap, we discussed this in the four cycles of learning in Chapter 8 (see pages 139–40).

Plug the gaps

I love this quote by John Donne and it's one I wholeheartedly live by, 'No (wo)man is an Island, entire of itself; every (wo)man is a piece of the Continent, a part of the main.' Relationships are the key to flourishing. Creating a rich network of confidants, loved ones, friends and mentors is the key to this work- and life-happiness puzzle. We will be discussing this later on.

Your words
When it comes to achieving what matters to you most, mastering your internal monologue will either help or hinder you when facing challenges, setbacks and plateaus. How can you challenge the stories that hold you back, practise self-compassion and quieten down your 'internal negative gremlin' from Chapter 2?

I've been slowly dousing you with BE HAPPY FIRST goodness throughout this book but for the purpose of this chapter, I think it's important to highlight two of the seven now. To find out more about the others, check out the resources at www.loveitleaveit.co.

First up PLUG THE GAPS.

Relationships and connections help to:

- Shape and refine you
- Act as mirrors of behaviours that you need to address, change or welcome
- Provide a space for you to develop emotionally and better articulate your thoughts and ideas

When I look at the relationships I have in my life, I'm lucky to have confidants, soulmates and friends who I can call on for support and advice at 3am. These people bring me joy, offer useful critique when I need it and help me feel powerful when I'm weak and perhaps in a place of self-doubt.

Think of the top five people in your life (partners, family, friends, co-workers).

- How do they support you?
- What do you feel is missing in your support system and how will you find it?
- Which relationships do you want to focus on more? Have you neglected some relationships in the midst of your work woes?

Hey, I need a little help

You may have some great friends and family members who can give you support and good life advice, but what about finding a replica in your professional life? How quickly could you go from having no job on a Wednesday to multiple opportunities and a job offer by the following week?

I ask you this because your ability to build honest connections will be your superhero strength to manoeuvre through the work-happiness maze. Whether you want to shift departments, start a business or move industries, taking the time to build a solid professional network always helps. Who do you have in your network? I suggest you start an inventory:

Potential mentors:

- People doing work you admire that you would like to pursue. With my help, they'll become your mentors soon!
- People in roles you are intrigued by, who may be open to you shadowing them and demystifying the role you hope to move into
- People you have second or third connections with on LinkedIn – the connection is lukewarm, but they have made career moves that match your own aspirations

Personal board of advisors:
A selection of unique individuals whom you can consult with, bounce ideas off and, in some cases, can help you make additional connections. For me, these have been past mentors, trusted friends, ex-coaches I paid to work with and LinkedIn connections that I reached out to. Whether you meet in person or virtually, or just check in with each other once a quarter or in times of transition, it's a mutually beneficial relationship. I'm always prepared to give back and do what I can in return to help them. Make sure your board of advisors, whether you have three or seven, are:

- Diverse – I've found power in the insight that comes from talking to people who have a diverse background of experience to draw from
- Progressive and action-oriented – it pays to connect with people who are drawn to forward momentum in their lives and work – it will rub off on you too

- Intelligent – I love talking to people smarter than me, it encourages me to stay curious, keep learning and debate differing opinions and ideas
- Good coaches – it's not always about telling you what to do. These individuals should be able to bring the best out of you and ask some provocative questions
- Excellent communicators – this goes without saying. If they can't distil ideas or articulate their thoughts, it's not helpful for either of you
- Networked – having a strategic advisor who can connect you with the right people and resources to help expand and build on your vision faster is crucial
- Experienced – it would be like the blind leading the blind if all your advisors didn't have credible experience or a strong track record in the areas you require

How do we begin the process of finding one of these treasured mentors? Have a look at the following example.

Emailing an expert you don't know

Hi Jenny

Greetings from a fellow University of Manchester alumnus. I was researching Creative Producer positions on LinkedIn, and I noticed you're a producer at Google doing some incredible and award-winning work.

I'm on a quest for my dream job and would love to ask you some questions about your experience as a producer and your time in a company like Google.

Would you be available for a quick chat over coffee this Thursday at 10am? I'm also free any time on Friday. Equally, if it's easier for you, I'd be happy to send my questions via email.

Yours sincerely,

Jessica

Tips for making super connections

- Explain the reasons why you are inspired by them and what you admire; pay them an honest compliment
- Be specific with your request and make it easy for them to say yes
- Ask open-ended questions: I'm actually interested in shifting roles – going from straight [account management] into [creative producer]. Obviously that's a big change, but I do have some experience in my last job doing X, Y and Z. Do you think that experience would be directly applicable to this position? How should I approach creative producer jobs if I apply for them?
- If you do end up meeting, respect their time
- Send thank-you notes or emails or gifts; it's important to let them know the impact the conversation had on you and the action you have taken
- Report back on progress – let them know you've made a connection with someone they suggested
- Add value – reciprocate, reciprocate, reciprocate. This isn't a one-way street. For example, 'I saw this article in *Creative Review* and it reminded me of what you said about the power of innovation hubs. No response needed. I just thought you might find it interesting.'

I reached out to Natalie Campbell, who balances an incredible portfolio of work as an award-winning serial social entrepreneur and board member across various institutions. She's achieved great success through grit, vision and the power of her support network.

'Mentors and people who will back and sponsor you throughout your career are integral to professional success. As a cornerstone of advice and an honest cheerleader, the people you choose to be a part of your journey are the difference between getting through a tough decision and letting tough decisions get the best of you. It's never too early to start, teachers are mentors and sponsors in the way they behave, put us forward for awards, select us for sports teams and pull us to one side to say "buck up your ideas" and "well

done, I know you worked hard". It's the same whether you are 15, 25 or 55. Find people in your corner, no matter what.'

Natalie Campbell, social entrepreneur

Building your work-happiness support systems isn't going to happen overnight – it takes time and patience. You need to keep acting on the advice your mentors give you and keep providing them with value too, so that it feels like you are both getting great benefits. But it will be worth it in the end.

Seeing the brighter side

The last step in BE HAPPY FIRST is mastering Your Words – your internal monologue. I think it's important to look at how our words can make or break our success, frame our idea of failure and help us take on our work changes with grace.

Failure

'What did you fail at this week?' I heard Sara Blakely of Spanx talk about how her dad would ask her this question at the dinner table each week so that they could learn the value of failure. The beauty of this question over 'How was your week?' means that we have to get close and comfortable with failure, evaluate it with a different lens and change our vocabulary around it.

EXERCISE

F**k fear and do it anyway

Overcoming the angst of potential mistakes

With lots of potential next moves or forks in the road, we can become frozen for fear of making mistakes. I want you to jot down:

What dream or action step would I like to bring to life or try?	What are my immediate fears or worst-case scenarios?	What's the best outcome that could happen?	What first steps will I try?
Move from officer manager into property developing.	I don't have any knowledge. I'll lose money. I'll buy the wrong property.	I could use my organizational skills to coordinate a team. I will research to find the best options.	I will start in the evenings after work and attend an auction this Saturday to get some experience and meet people to build a team.

'You might never fail on the scale I did, but some failure in life is inevitable. It is impossible to live without failing at something, unless you live so cautiously that you might as well not have lived at all – in which case, you fail by default.'

J.K. Rowling

Rather than letting fear of the unknown or of not being good enough dictate your next move or decisions, use inexperience and perceived weaknesses to your advantage to set you up for success.

Reframing the failure

What if you do make a mistake? Let's look at how you can reframe your attitude towards things that haven't worked out or been an immediate success.

With the rise of Instagram and various social media platforms, most of us are just sharing the highlighted edits of our life, stripping away the bad bits and only posting the glamorous moments.

As Elizabeth Day, author and podcaster of *How to Fail with Elizabeth Day*, states, in a climate where success is the all-consuming aspiration, it becomes increasingly difficult to try new things or take risks. But failure has taught me lessons I would never otherwise have understood. We rarely share the business idea that tanked or the fears of balancing credit cards every month to make ends meet but when you do, you can start to dissect the learnings and foresee obstacles that will help you to future-proof the next pivot or iteration of your career.

EXERCISE

The silver lining

Use this table to help you identify how to change your perspective on failure and what you can learn from it.

Perceived or known failure	What really happened?	What was the opportunity or success from this perceived failure?
I failed to launch a shoe business.	Timing and money didn't align.	I used my design and fashion skills to start a personal branding business which led to my next career move.
I didn't get the job because I'm useless.	The role required more advanced-level experience.	I will seek training to acquire this new skill set.

Bridging the gaps in your CV

Making changes around your work or leaving a job is difficult for two reasons. We can become anxious at the prospect of trying to explain changes in direction, work gaps and dips. Try to set that anxiety aside and think about how you would answer these questions:

- Why do you want to jump from where you are to this new job?
- What were you doing between the years X and Y. Why the gap?

The more adaptable and open you are about your 'work story', the more you will be able to answer these questions convincingly and with ease, allowing you to grab opportunities. In order to get over one job and move on to another, you have to do an audit of where you are, where you want to get to and what you need to take you there. Invest in a better viewpoint.

Here are a few scenarios:

Scenario 1: Why did you leave this role/company?

- What might look like a golden opportunity to some could be a nightmare to others, so be clear on why you have made certain dynamic changes, what the gains were and what you hope to deliver to the company you are interviewing with as a result of these changes
- Maybe you decided to take a 'Mintern', as the BBC puts it, quitting your job to either retrain or take an internship in your new, chosen field, starting from the bottom in your mid- to late-30s
- Perhaps you were in quite a senior position which you felt didn't make the best use of your skills or would take you towards your desired career and life-happiness direction

Scenario 2: What happened between 2012 and 2014?

- Try to articulate what actually happened in the gap that would be positive and beneficial to the company
- Perhaps you took a sabbatical to travel and learn a new language?

Maybe you went back to study or retrain? You can explain how you are now ready to put that to use in your new role

- Perhaps you had a baby, looked after an ageing parent or had a period of sickness? Life moments and events happen, you are only human! Explaining with honesty and authenticity always trumps making up a cover story

Scenario 3: Why have you jumped from one sector to another and back again?

- Perhaps it gave you an opportunity to build new skills and strengths? To rediscover the joy you had for the old sector by trialling something new? The different work environments helped you build stronger interpersonal skills and relationships? The knowledge from both sectors gives you an advantage?

Rather than doubt your career moves or worry about what people think, note how you've grown and what you've collected by way of experiences, skills and tools, and how this will feed your future moves. This is pivotal to becoming more confident and preparing yourself for tricky questions.

Grieving your work changes

Making changes in our work life can be difficult because of all the deep-rooted experiences and memories we may have about our job. We may have made some lifelong friends or maybe we met our partner there. The memories might have been confidence-deflating (toxic boss/culture/workmates or embarrassing work presentations) or enhancing (promotions/recognition). When we leave one place or a department, we face that scary prospect of not knowing what we will run into next and battling our internal imposter syndrome about whether we can deliver results again in a new space.

Some of my clients grieve for jobs they didn't even like – they were in a job for a long time and the routine became their crutch. It's easy to get stuck in a way of showing up that's comfortable and hard to shift.

When it comes to thinking about the people you care about, decide who you will truly keep in contact with and say thank you to those you leave behind and those whom you enjoyed working with.

Once you've handed in your notice and left, it's important to package up your emotions or grief around your past role before you start the new one, even if you remain in the same company but have just moved departments or teams. Just like relationships, you shouldn't bring old baggage into the new one. You might still be unpicking a few memories from your old job in the early days of a new gig, but realistically no one wants to hear about what went badly. Go in with an open mind and spirit. Let it surprise and delight you.

Now what?

The troublesome trio of money, networking and owning your work story are some of the biggest challenges that stand in the way of finding work happiness. By working through the exercises in this chapter, you are giving yourself a greater chance of making a successful change.

If you do need an extra nudge, join me in the final chapter for some words that I live by, that keep me moving forwards towards my goals even when I can't see the road ahead.

Visit www.loveitleaveit.co for additional resources, tools, templates and book recommendations for this chapter.

CHAPTER 12

THE TIME IS NOW!

I was once asked to give a talk on the topic of 'living with purpose and ageing with pride and agency'. It got me thinking about my life up until now, as a 38-year-old woman (at the time of writing). I thought about how my life has been intertwined with life and death since I was young and how it's unknowingly channelled my purpose and my relationship to work.

You know my story already, so I won't rehash the work journey again, but I want to explain how my personal journey evolved alongside it. I was brought into hospital at the age of five with a case of meningitis and pneumonia and, when I wasn't responding to antibiotics and getting rapidly worse, they investigated a little further and then boom! I was diagnosed with sickle-cell anaemia. I remember very vividly lying in bed looking at my Dad tearing up and my Mum looking dumbstruck at the doctor as he described my diagnosis, stating that most children with this chronic illness don't make it to adulthood.

As I grew up, my mum would always remind me of how lucky I was: 'Sammy, you were meant to be here for a purpose.' In my mid-teens, I couldn't quite see the purpose. All I could see was how annoyed I was at not being able to do things like the other kids. As I grew up, I suffered more and more from bouts of sickle cell crisis. First when I was five, then when I was stuck in hospital during university while everyone was enjoying student life and I was hooked up to a drip, and finally when I decided to escape the grips of the British winter for seven weeks' respite in Brazil only to get sick on a solo part of a group trip. I was writhing in pain in a Brazilian hospital, unable to speak a word of Portuguese and contemplating how friends and family would learn about my death.

In each of these moments, after the initial anger, frustration and tears, I would ask myself: what is this moment trying to teach me? What had I done in my life that would really matter if I died? With all of these lucky escapes, was I making use of the fact that I've lived past the prognosis? This isn't your average self-reflection, I admit.

As I worked in different companies, the brushes with sickness prevented me from delivering my best and I came to a point where I thought: enough is enough. Not only was I not happy doing the work, the environments I was working in weren't helping me and my body.

I made a pact to craft a better way of working that would coincide nicely with my mental and physical needs and bring to life the gifts in me that I could use to help others. Being called a supporter and a bright light by friends and family was one thing, but I wanted to help other people. Many of the steps in my journey to becoming a happiness consultant have been marred with sickness, pain, upset and frustration, but I've been sustained by a mission to empower others to push through barriers and find the resolve to try new things so that they too can live with intention and purpose.

As you mull over your decisions, I want you to embrace the idea of 'memento mori', which means 'remember that you will die'. You might think this is getting a bit morbid, but I want you to measure your next steps so that you choose wisely. I don't want you to miss out on an opportunity to make your life better today *and not tomorrow.*

The famous stoic, Seneca, wrote: 'Let us prepare our minds as if we'd come to the very end of life. Let us postpone nothing. Let us balance life's books each day... The one who puts the finishing touches on their life each day is never short of time.' This isn't just a stoic way of thinking. This approach has roots in Egyptian, Buddhist, Roman and Catholic teachings. Entrepreneurs, sports professionals and scholars of our time have used its meaning to spur them into action and maintain their forward momentum. All I'm asking is that you think about the spark that will light your fire and allow you to embrace all opportunities.

As Shunryu Suzuki, founding father of Zen Buddhism in the US, states: 'in the beginner's mind there are many possibilities, but in the expert's there are few'; that's all I'm asking you to think about.

So what's it going to be?

Whether you choose to 'Love It' or 'Leave It', don't wait in vain. My hope is that this book has guided you to think, see and act differently when it comes to your work happiness.

Use what you have read to be specific about what you want. Avoid keeping your options open – even if you make the wrong decision you are still making a decision and moving forwards. Think back to where you were a year ago today and then imagine where you'll be eight weeks, six months or even a year from now with all this new panache, insight, knowledge and swagger. I always ask my clients what will hurt them the most:

Settling for a stressful, unhappy and demoralizing work life

Or

Putting up with a bit of discomfort as you work out what really makes you happy in life and at work.

Love it or leave it…?

The 'four office characters' quiz

In Chapter 4 we first introduced four tricky characters who you may come across at work, and in Chapter 7 we discussed how to start building better relationships with each of these characters to help you feel happier at work. To identify which profile you are, answer each of the following questions by noting down which answer resonates the most. At the end, count up how many of each letter you have to discover which character fits your profile.

1.

At work, in your day-to-day activities and tasks, the priorities that matter most to you are:

A. To achieve great results, overcome obstacles and celebrate wins.

B. To feel respected, work on multiple things with people and to be liked.

C. To create a serene environment and a set of processes and systems for people to excel in and do their best work.

D. To work in an orderly fashion without spontaneous surprises or time pressures on my own.

At work, in your day-to-day activities and tasks, the priorities that matter least to you are:

A. To work in an orderly fashion without spontaneous surprises or time pressures on my own.

B. To create a serene environment and a set of processes and systems for people to excel in and do their best work.

C. To achieve great results, overcome obstacles and celebrate wins.

D. To feel respected, work on multiple things with people and to be liked.

2.

Working in a team, you are most likely to be the one who:

A. Is ready to start immediately; less talk more action.

B. Makes the time fly with jokes, humour and fun.

C. Is interested in getting everyone involved, even the silent ones.

D. Will charge forward once a plan is in place.

Working in a team, you are least likely to be the one who:

A. Makes the time fly with jokes, humour and fun.

B. Will charge forward once a plan is in place.

C. Is ready to start immediately; less talk more action.

D. Is interested in getting everyone involved, even the silent ones.

3.

If someone says something that you disagree with, what are you most likely to do or say?

A. Be radically honest and tell them you don't agree.

B. Become curious and ask them to explain further.

C. Change the tone or subject.

D. Appear nonchalent.

If someone says something that you disagree with, what are you least likely to do or say?

A. Appear nonchalent.

B. Change the tone or subject.

C. Be radically honest and tell them you don't agree.

D. Become curious and ask them to explain further.

4.

When it comes to free-form work such as researching, brainstorming sessions, creative visualizing, what is your attitude most likely to be?

A. Fab, if it gets us to the end goal quickly.

B. Great, if it brings everyone together, I'm open to it.

C. I enjoy this kind of work a lot.

D. I'm open to it if it helps the wider team to problem-solve.

When it comes to free-form work such as researching, brainstorming sessions, creative visualizing, what is your attitude least likely to be?

A. I enjoy this kind of work a lot.

B. I'm open to it if it helps the wider team to problem-solve.

C. Fab, if it gets us to the end goal quickly.

D. Great, if it brings everyone together, I'm open to it.

5.

What are you most likely to say or do when you encounter a problem?

A. Forget procrastination, you will choose a path forward and get on with it pronto.

B. Know that it will all be OK, so there is no point in worrying.

C. Analyse your feelings and make an emotional decision.

D. Get more data and facts so that you can carefully map out all options.

What are you least likely to say or do when you encounter a problem?

A. Know that it will all be OK, so there is no point in worrying.

B. Get more data and facts so that you can carefully map out all options.

C. Forget procrastination, you will choose a path forward and get on with it pronto.

D. Analyse your feelings and make an emotional decision.

6.

At a networking event, you are most likely to:

A. Connect with people in a fun and unique way that goes beyond 'What do you do?'

B. Keep calm, observe and find small pockets of people to get to know.

C. Follow a strict plan to collect details of a set number of people in optimum time.

D. Prior to the event, research the key people to find, meet and connect with them, then leave.

At a networking event, you are least likely to:

A. Keep calm, observe and find small pockets of people to get to know and provide value.

B. Follow a strict plan to collect details of a set number of people.

C. Prior to the event, research the key people to find, meet and connect with them, then leave.

D. Connect with people in a fun and unique way that goes beyond 'What do you do?'

7.

The key types of work that you enjoy most are:

A. Progressive and fast-paced tasks that lead to success for me and my teams.

B. Meeting new people, getting new ideas, sparking bright ideas.

C. Solitary and autonomous work.

D. Repetitive, predictable tasks.

The key types of work that you enjoy least are:

A. Meeting new people, getting new ideas, sparking bright ideas.

B. Solitary and autonomous work.

C. Repetitive, predictable tasks.

D. Progressive and fast-paced tasks that lead to success for me and my teams.

8.

You would describe yourself mostly as:

A. Driven, competent, results-oriented

B. Guider, sociable, outgoing

C. Kind, considered and a peacekeeper

D. Methodical, precise, efficient

You would describe yourself least as:

A. Kind, considered and a peacekeeper

B. Driven, competent, results-oriented

C. Methodical, precise, efficient

D. Guider, sociable, outgoing

9.

When people come over to talk to you about a project, you are mostly interested in:

A. Talking to the person leading the project.

B. Understanding what new ideas you can contribute.

C. Identifying how this project has a wider ripple effect.

D. Understanding why and how you are needed.

When people come over to talk to you about a project, you are least interested in:

A. Identifying how this project has a wider ripple effect.

B. Understanding why and how you are needed on this project.

C. Understanding what new ideas you can contribute.

D. Talking to the person leading the project.

10.

When you hear about sudden change, you are most likely to think:

A. How will it shape my ability to achieve results?

B. How is this going to shape my experience?

C. What will this do to everyone else?

D. What's the best way to map it out?

When you hear about sudden change, you are least likely to think:

A. What will this do to everyone else?

B. What's the best way to map it out?

C. How will it shape my ability to achieve results?

D. How is this going to shape my experience?

11.

What is the best thing someone could say to you?

A. You always achieve results.

B. We missed your presence at the meeting/office/party yesterday.

C. I always feel seen and heard by you.

D. Wow, you've completed so much in such a short time.

What is the worst thing someone could say to you?

A. I always feel seen and heard by you.

B. Wow, you've completed so much in such a short time.

C. You always achieve results.

D. We missed your presence at the meeting/office/party yesterday.

12.

This is how you are most likely to approach work or a project:

A. Get consensus on the best approach forward.

B. Find someone to partner with.

C. Gain more knowledge into the end goal before I start.

D. Work through my to-do list in a quick and succinct manner.

This is how you are least likely to approach work or a project:

A. Find someone to partner with.

B. Get consensus on the best approach forward.

C. Work through my to-do list in a quick and succinct manner.

D. Gain more knowledge into the end goal before I start.

If you scored...

Mostly As
Commander
This describes the way you deal with problems – by asserting yourself and controlling situations. You like to get work done and achieve results and big wins.

Mostly Bs
Navigator
This describes the way you deal with people – the way you communicate and relate to others. You like to engage with many, to enjoy the process and be energized by new ideas.

Mostly Cs
Pacifier
This describes your temperament – patient, persistent and thoughtful. You like to make sure people feel welcomed, engaged and heard.

Mostly Ds
Cautious
This describes how you approach and organize your activity, procedures and responsibilities. You value solo time to work in your own autonomous way.

APPENDIX II

Strengths test

Now it's time to find your superhero strengths. Each zone has a set of five questions. Mark how you feel about each statement using the following:

- ➤ Highly Agree = 5 points
- ➤ Mildly Agree = 4 points
- ➤ Neutral = 3 points
- ➤ Mildly Disagree = 2 points
- ➤ Highly Disagree = 1 point

At the end of each zone, mark up your total and note down the scores – I've filled in the first zone as an example. Once you have the scores for all your zones, you can check the results to pinpoint your top five superhero strength zones.

Zone 1 – Polymath

Statement	Highly agree (5)	Mildly agree (4)	Neutral (3)	Mildly disagree (2)	Highly disagree (1)
1. I get bored quickly if there is no scope to learn new things	x				
2. I have no problem picking up new concepts quickly		x			
3. I believe it's better to be a generalist than a specialist			x		
4. It's energizing for me to learn something new, regardless of what it is					x
5. My enthusiasm and thirst for knowledge is contagious and admirable		x			

Total score for ZONE 1 = 17 (5+4+3+1+4)

Zone 2 – Narrator

Statement	Highly agree (5)	Mildly agree (4)	Neutral (3)	Mildly disagree (2)	Highly disagree (1)
6. The best way to share your point of view is to tell a story					
7. My friends say that I can make an 'adventure' out of any mundane event					
8. People are naturally captivated by what I have to say					
9. It gives me pleasure to use words in a unique way to share a message					
10. Public speaking comes naturally to me					

Zone 3 – Firestarter

Statement	Highly agree (5)	Mildly agree (4)	Neutral (3)	Mildly disagree (2)	Highly disagree (1)
11. I love starting something new and not necessarily be the one to finish it					
12. I like to get the wheels turning on new projects, ideas and opportunities					
13. I believe that by asking thought-provoking questions, you can achieve great solutions					
14. Implementation is great, but it all starts with a brilliant idea					
15. All talk and no action makes me irritable					

Zone 4 – Balancer

Statement	Highly agree (5)	Mildly agree (4)	Neutral (3)	Mildly disagree (2)	Highly disagree (1)
16. It's better to create peace than fuel continuous, unnecessary conflict					
17. Harmony creates successful productivity					
18. I love creating peace between two people with divergent viewpoints					
19. I take it upon myself to include everyone and make sure all are treated fairly					
20. I like to understand both sides of every argument					

Zone 5 – Tactical

Statement	Highly agree (5)	Mildly agree (4)	Neutral (3)	Mildly disagree (2)	Highly disagree (1)
21. It's challenging for me to work with people who can't see the bigger picture					
22. I hate focusing on small details					
23. I like to think several steps ahead					
24. It's easy for me to see similarities in seemingly different and complex problems					
25. I believe you can't solve new problems with old solutions, you need fresh thinking					

Zone 6 – Braniac

Statement	Highly agree (5)	Mildly agree (4)	Neutral (3)	Mildly disagree (2)	Highly disagree (1)
26. I need time and space to think before I reach any conclusions					
27. I often get lost in my mind and thoughts					
28. My friends often marvel at my depth and breadth of thinking					
29. Theory is a useful foundation for any practice or action					
30. I get excited by time alone to reflect					

Zone 7 – Rapport builder

Statement	Highly agree (5)	Mildly agree (4)	Neutral (3)	Mildly disagree (2)	Highly disagree (1)
31. I am often called upon to smooth out conflicts					
32. I am able to understand the needs of others without them uttering a word					
33. I always seek common ground and understanding with all that I meet					
34. People naturally feel understood and cared for in my presence					
35. While I may not agree with everyone, I can always comprehend how people may feel					

Zone 8 – Acrobat

Statement	Highly agree (5)	Mildly agree (4)	Neutral (3)	Mildly disagree (2)	Highly disagree (1)
36. I find it easy to adjust to change					
37. I love curveballs, sudden changes and chaos					
38. Flexibility makes me excited over solid commitments					
39. I'm a pretty malleable and easy-going person					
40. Too much consistency and predictability is boring to me					

Zone 9 – Leader

Statement	Highly agree (5)	Mildly agree (4)	Neutral (3)	Mildly disagree (2)	Highly disagree (1)
41. I like to bring order to situations that seem chaotic					
42. People get excited when I take charge					
43. I feel exhilarated when people implement my orders					
44. I exude a level of certainty and confidence					
45. I feel comfortable sharing views that may unsettle people					

Zone 10 – Evaluator

Statement	Highly agree (5)	Mildly agree (4)	Neutral (3)	Mildly disagree (2)	Highly disagree (1)
46. Give me solid facts over whimsical thinking					
47. People call me logical and precise					
48. I hate mixing emotions and logic; logic always wins for me					
49. If you have a point to make, it's always best to do it with cold, hard facts and numbers					
50. Nothing brings me more joy than numbers and data					

Zone 11 – Conqueror

Statement	Highly agree (5)	Mildly agree (4)	Neutral (3)	Mildly disagree (2)	Highly disagree (1)
51. Success is important to me					
52. My friends say that I am naturally competitive					
53. Competition is the best way to bring out determination and excellence in anyone					
54. I like to win, competitions, arguments, board games... you name it!					
55. I compete with others to push myself harder					

Zone 12 – Fixer

Statement	Highly agree (5)	Mildly agree (4)	Neutral (3)	Mildly disagree (2)	Highly disagree (1)
56. Every day there are problems waiting to be fixed					
57. Nothing excites me more than fixing a problem that has defeated others					
58. People always come to me to help them get unstuck					
59. Nothing is impossible to solve					
60. Finding solutions comes easily to me					

Zone 13 – Mentor

Statement	Highly agree (5)	Mildly agree (4)	Neutral (3)	Mildly disagree (2)	Highly disagree (1)
61. I love being a supporter for change in others					
62. We should all help those around us to fulfil their potential					
63. I want people to win and achieve success					
64. I like to remove obstacles that stop people from succeeding					
65. I'm naturally inclined to want to help people excel					

Zone 14 – Virtuous

Statement	Highly agree (5)	Mildly agree (4)	Neutral (3)	Mildly disagree (2)	Highly disagree (1)
66. The worst thing for me is to feel that my values are being compromised					
67. I am guided by a strong sense of purpose					
68. I won't compromise my standards for anyone					
69. I believe actions say a lot about what a person stands for					
70. I expect others to respect my values just as much as I respect theirs					

Zone 15 – Creator

Statement	Highly agree (5)	Mildly agree (4)	Neutral (3)	Mildly disagree (2)	Highly disagree (1)
71. I feel excited when I have the freedom to create without limitation					
72. People always come to me for fresh, innovative ideas					
73. Every day I come up with more new ideas					
74. I like to push people to come up with better ideas					
75. I become impatient when people don't use their imagination					

Zone 16 – Solo warrior

Statement	Highly agree (5)	Mildly agree (4)	Neutral (3)	Mildly disagree (2)	Highly disagree (1)
76. I like coming to decisions in my own time without people forcing me					
77. I have absolute trust in my abilities, intuition and myself					
78. I love that I have the power to determine my reality					
79. I trust myself to always make the right decision					
80. People admire my strong sense of self					

Zone 17 – Hopeful

Statement	Highly agree (5)	Mildly agree (4)	Neutral (3)	Mildly disagree (2)	Highly disagree (1)
81. It frustrates me when people pick holes in every situation					
82. I'd rather see the glass as half full than half empty					
83. I always look for the positive in my work and life					
84. I'd rather think the best of people than the worst					
85. Even in dark times there is always the opportunity to find happiness					

Zone 18 – Committed

Statement	Highly agree (5)	Mildly agree (4)	Neutral (3)	Mildly disagree (2)	Highly disagree (1)
86. My eye is always on the end goal					
87. I think it's important to follow through on a commitment, no matter how big or small					
88. I expect others to be as committed to their actions and values as I am					
89. I love delivering on what I have promised to do					
90. Reputation is built on your ability to meet your commitments					

Zone 19 – Methodical

Statement	Highly agree (5)	Mildly agree (4)	Neutral (3)	Mildly disagree (2)	Highly disagree (1)
91. I love routine, schedules and deadlines					
92. There is nothing I like more than being reliable					
93. I believe success comes from following a specific roadmap					
94. I hate it when people don't stick to a plan					
95. Without a plan I feel lost					

Zone 20 – Considered

Statement	Highly agree (5)	Mildly agree (4)	Neutral (3)	Mildly disagree (2)	Highly disagree (1)
96. I like to focus on one thing at a time					
97. Distractions and multitasking make me feel queasy					
98. People say that I evaluate every task and action meticulously					
99. It frustrates me when people act without careful consideration of their actions					
100. I'd rather be slow and steady in my actions so as to avoid making mistakes					

Results

Add up the scores across each of your zones – you will start to see which ones rank the highest for you. What are your top five superhero strength zones?

Zone 1: Polymath Learning is so sexy to you! Waxing lyrical on new subjects, random pieces of knowledge and facts fills you with glee.	**Zone 8: Acrobat** Whatever the situation, you can adapt, shapeshift, balance or mould yourself to it. You hate being boxed in.
Zone 2: Narrator Let me take you on a journey! Always one to craft an epic story out of the mundane to surprise and delight any audience.	**Zone 9: Leader** You always put your hands up first, ready to highlight the best way forward. You can always rally people towards a common goal.
Zone 3: Fire-starter Anyone need a lighter? You've got the power to ignite new creativity or inject innovation into tired situations or ways of thinking.	**Zone 10: Evaluator** Facts, data and numbers give you the confidence to make clear and effective decisions. You have a strong analytical mind.
Zone 4: Balancer You like helping people to reach a compromise for the greater good. Peace is what you seek and you strive to help create that in times of tension and discord.	**Zone 11: Conqueror** You are a natural competitor and driven by a determination to excel. Success is more than just coming in first to you, it's about making sure you employ your skills to the best use possible.
Zone 5: Tactical You are logical and strategic. You love to cut through the crap to get to a decision and provide everyone with a roadmap.	**Zone 12: Fixer** Fixing problems makes your heart sing! You don't shy away from a messy situation or issue that needs solving.
Zone 6: Brainiac A deep thinker, you like to reflect on great ideas and solutions before making decisions.	**Zone 13: Mentor** Potential is like a hidden gem that you like to unearth in other people. Through asking questions and being curious, you coax and tease out people's hidden talents to help them excel.
Zone 7: Rapport builder You love nothing better than appreciating and understanding how others feel and doing what you can to make sure they always feel positive.	**Zone 14: Virtuous** You are upstanding, with high moral standards that you won't compromise for anyone. Working in scenarios that compromise your values feels like a drag.

Zone 15: Creator Always brimming with radical suggestions, new objectives, recommendations and goals.	**Zone 18: Committed** You love to keep your promises! You believe that actions matter most and you hate to disappoint others without good reason. If you say you'll do something, you will never be flimsy with your word
Zone 16: Solo warrior I don't need any help! That's often your first and last thought. You prefer to satisfy your needs without outside interference.	**Zone 19: Methodical** Did someone say spreadsheet, to-do lists and project plans? These are your guilty pleasures that help you achieve your goals.
Zone 17: Hopeful Always looking on the bright side and seeing optimism at every angle.	**Zone 20: Considered** One foot in front of the other for you. No point rushing yourself, you enjoy taking your time, cogitating over one problem at a time. Your plans are well thought through.

APPENDIX III

Excuse me, I'd like to have a word...

Throughout the book I've been giving you helpful exercises to aid your decision about what path is right for you, whether 'Love It' or 'Leave It'. Perhaps you are a little clearer on your direction, but maybe having conversations about working hours with your manager or approaching your partner still seem quite daunting. Here are a series of tried-and-tested tips and scripts to help with some tricky conversations such as:

- ➤ Starting a conversation with your partner about potential work changes
- ➤ Negotiating the terms of your current role to work from home or part-time
- ➤ Requesting a six-week sabbatical
- ➤ Approaching your manager about more ways to increase happiness at work

Dive in and start making some changes today.

Starting a conversation with your partner about work changes

I decided to interview Lotte Jeffs, an award-winning journalist, magazine editor, author and advertising creative director, on the rigours of work-happiness conversations with your partner and how to navigate this.

What's the best way to communicate with your partner about a career transition you want to make?

I think you need to not be selfish and weigh up the impact this decision will have on the other important people in your life. Relocating, spending more time apart, anticipating worse benefits or a drop in salary are all things that involve more than just you, so I'd advise having a conversation about your career transition before you make any decision. Explain your idea and thinking, and ask what your partner feels about it. And genuinely listen and care about their answer. I'd also advise having small, regular chats about something like this whenever you can, as and when you think about it, and involve your partner in these early percolating stages rather than having one big weighty conversation where you've done a lot of thinking on your own but not shared the process – that can feel like a bombshell and lead to an argument.

How do couples prepare for when both partners want to make big career shifts such as starting a business and freelancing?

Welcome to my life! It takes a lot of organization, openness and willingness to compromise. Make sure you feel that you are being given equal time and space to build your career rather than seethe with resentment if you think your partner has more time than you. Coming from a place of absolute equality, where both of your careers are equally important and there are no gendered expectations around who should have the 'star' career, is a healthy basis from which to have these kinds of discussions. Also, be realistic and not selfish. Is it genuinely going to be possible for both of you to take a big professional leap at the same time? Perhaps you would be better off as a family if you staggered it. Again, it comes down to talking openly and often.

What's the best way to discuss money and earnings with your partner during times of career transition?
Just do it. If you pussyfoot around the subject, you make it weird and complicated when it doesn't need to be. You need to make sure that you are both contributing fairly to the household, based on what you can afford, and the only way to do that is to be honest about how much you are earning and what will need to change if you make a career transition.

How can you keep cheerleading your partner, even if it means your progression may be slightly different or staggered? How do you make peace with the journey?
Having a shared plan helps. Knowing that next month or year it will be your partner's turn to quit their job and follow their dream means you can plan accordingly. Think about your quality of life and what really makes you happy, and build your professional lives around that and not the other way round. Enjoy the moment. If you've taken time off to raise your child, enjoy that as another step in your portfolio of life and work, rather than focusing on what you might be missing in a professional sense. It can be hard, particularly if you are very professionally ambitious, to let yourself 'lean out' for a while, but relax into whatever this new role might be rather than fight it and be generous in supporting each other through all your different life and career moments.

Negotiating the terms of your current role to work from home or part-time

Step 1: Know thyself

Before you ask your boss to work from home, make sure you can follow through on your promises. Give serious consideration to the pros and cons. Do you have a reliable computer and an internet connection? Will you be able to get stuff done if you're not in the office every day? Have you got a good home office that will support your productivity and wellbeing? Be realistic here! If you have young children at home, how will you navigate hopping on last-minute video calls? It's also important to know how you will create some differentiation between work and rest, otherwise it all gets a bit blurry and you may find it hard to know when work starts and stops.

Step 2: Prepare your case

Do other workers work remotely on an occasional basis? If so, think about how allowing them to do so provides a benefit to the company. If you're proposing something brand new, be prepared to spend more time and energy building your case. Equally, don't throw your toys out of the pram if you don't succeed the first time you ask. Flexibility and patience are vital when you are trying to convince management to make big changes.

Step 3: Zone in on the positives

Would skipping the commute allow you to start earlier? Are there other ways that working from home could make or save the company money? Be as specific as possible and provide a strategic plan outlining the benefits and value to **your employer (not yourself)**.

Step 4: Stamp out any concerns

In any negotiation, it pays to be one step ahead of potential concerns. When you're putting in a request like this, be sure to mention how you will get your job responsibilities done. Outline for your employer what your new schedule would look like. Provide your manager with viable options that would work to ensure uninterrupted staff coverage.

Step 5: Suggest a trial

Many managers understandably want to see results before committing to more flexible working. If your boss seems willing, suggest a trial basis. Outline what you expect to accomplish and how you'll continue to provide the same level of work as you do in the office. Anticipate concerns about attending meetings, collaborating with teammates and being available by phone, email and messaging.

Requesting a six-week sabbatical

Step 1: Set the tone

It's best to start with a brief positioning statement regarding your career, your experience and your commitment to bringing value to your job. At this point it's useful to mention what else would enhance your current work experience and what gaps you think need filling to enhance your career growth and bring value to your team and department. Discuss that you have been looking into various options, one option being a short-term six-week sabbatical.

Step 2: The 'why'

Succinctly state the purpose of your sabbatical in a couple of sentences. What do you plan to do? Obviously they aren't going to allow you to go off on a paid holiday, so what will this sabbatical enable you to achieve and, again, what's the benefit for the company:

- ➤ Cultural immersion – will you learn a new language?
- ➤ Learning and development – is it a strategic bootcamp where you will learn to be a better leader or a wellbeing retreat to reset your focus, mind and body?
- ➤ Volunteering – whether it's building homes or working on an education project for young children, why do you want to spend your time volunteering?
- ➤ Remote working experience – perhaps you want the chance to mix with other employed individuals or entrepreneurs from all over the world as you travel to a new country to breathe new life into your own work, skills and outlook?

Step 3: What's the value to the company?

Briefly illustrate the benefits of your sabbatical. Again, step into the company's shoes and ask yourself: what's in it for them? If at all possible, link the purpose of your sabbatical to these benefits. List a few companies that offer sabbaticals (fully paid and unpaid so you can show variety). This can show your current company not only how widely it is practised, but also that such an offering will make them competitive in their field and also help attract younger talent. It's worth noting, if they do agree, whether you or they are prepared to accept it as unpaid.

Step 4: Delivered work

What do you hope to deliver on before you head off? This section is about demonstrating your value to your employer while providing positive checklists of all the areas you will have covered before you go.

Step 5: Work-coverage plan

This section is all about pre-empting the 'what about/what if...' questions. Who will cover your work in your absence and how? If you are open to allowing some time to work, how will you adhere to this across different time zones? Present problem-solving ideas for how work will be covered in your absence.

Step 6: Planned weeks of leave and accessibility during leave

What are the start and end dates of your sabbatical? Where do you plan to be and how might they contact you if a need arises?

Offering a limited level of access might help you get approval of your sabbatical from an otherwise reluctant manager, though it helps to set an expectation that accessibility will be minimal and no sooner than the end of the third or fourth week of your leave. If you'd rather not commit, then skip this but it could help your chances if your manager has some security knowing that they may be able to contact you in an emergency.

Step 7: Return to work and summary

Provide a short summary which clarifies your commitment to your job while inviting discussion of your proposal.

Below is an email template you can use to ask for a short-term sabbatical leave that can be sent to your manager or you can use some of the framework in a sit-down conversation.

Proposal for a short-term sabbatical leave

Having developed my career in [professional area] over [#] years, [#*] of them with [employer], I've acquired substantial knowledge and experience that continue to prove valuable in my current position. [*Your chances of proposal approval are best if this number is more than 5.]

My work [and achievements] at [employer] is [are] important to me and I expect to be an active employee for years to come.

I'm now at a stage in my work life where a period of renewal and personal development would benefit both me and the [name your department or work group]. By way of this proposal, I am making a formal request for a short-term sabbatical leave, beginning on [date; for about 6–9 months out or no sooner than 3 months from your proposal presentation].

I have an opportunity to [briefly describe your sabbatical plans and purpose].

This temporary shift from my regular work will recharge my creative thinking and renew my energy, bringing a fresh level of productivity and engagement to my role in the [name] department [work group] at [employer].

Insert some pithy research on the value of sabbaticals, such as:

- *Business Week* reports, 'Sabbaticals reduce turnover and retain wisdom otherwise lost when veteran employees burn out'
- Maybe add a stat here relating to the value of sabbaticals, how they help with alleviating stress, increasing creativity, etc…
- These employer payoffs are the key reasons why sabbaticals are offered by Nike, Adobe, Penguin Random House, Patagonia, Deloitte and many others

Work projects I plan to complete before the sabbatical start date:

- [Name the project. Describe the outcome and payoff to your manager/employer.]
- As above
- As above

I've given a lot of thought to how my high-priority work [and major projects] can be managed [or reassigned] during the time I'm away from the office. Below is a proposed plan for work coverage during my leave.

- [List your projects/responsibilities and a brief narrative on how they can be managed.]

[Key Colleague's name] has agreed to manage any [unlikely] urgent matters. [Note this is optional – consider whether it's best if you and your manager decide who will take over your duties together or if it's better for you to be proactive and make a suggestion.] Less critical job duties [such as…] can be deferred until my return.

The work-coverage plan outlined above covers a leave of [#] weeks, starting on [date], with a planned return-to-work date of [date]. This time off includes [#] weeks of projected accrued paid time off*. I am requesting [#] additional weeks to complete the sabbatical leave. [*Be ready to apply a week or more of your paid time off, but avoid using all of it.]

In line with the nature and purpose of a sabbatical leave, I'll refrain from checking in with the office until the week just prior to my planned return.

In addition to the Work-coverage Plan, [Key Colleague] has agreed to be my primary point of contact at the office. [This assumes someone other than your manager is a more prudent choice.] S/he will be well-equipped with documented procedures related to my work duties. In collaboration with you and others, s/he is willing to troubleshoot various situations that might arise and assess their urgency to determine whether or not I need to be contacted.

As a contingency, I've tested remote access software and arranged secure access to my computer and all its files from any internet connection in the world, should an urgent need require it. [Obviously this might be worded differently depending on your company's data policy.]

It's my intention to continue being a vital part of [department or work group] at [employer] for years to come. To cover the period of my planned absence, I offer this comprehensive proposal which considers both employer and employee needs.

I trust you'll agree that these arrangements are sufficient during my leave. I welcome your suggestions and your assistance in shaping the details. [This takes a bold 'assume the sale' approach.]

Want/need to start a 'Love It or Leave It' movement within your workplace?

You've read this book and you know in your heart, you need to start a Love It or Leave It (LILI) conversation of your own at work but feel unsure how. Here are a few ideas of how you could start to bring more happiness into your work as a team member or manager.

I'm a manager

As a manager, you have listened to your team and they are frustrated, burned out and in need of some support – and you are too. Without even knowing it, you hold a unique place within your company. You hear what the shop floor is saying AND you have access to more senior management conversations, so use make use of this!

Complete the starter happiness health check (overleaf) for yourself and at least five other colleagues (ideally from different departments and levels). Use the data you collect to give senior management an indicator of where current happiness levels are and this can then form the beginnings of a proposal to create a 'happiness team' dedicated to solving these problems. You can select someone in your team who is also passionate about the topic to generate initiatives and to share the work. If you're stuck for ideas, you can book a discovery session on how to run a longer Love It Leave It Health Check successfully in your company, see www.loveitleaveit.co/love-it-leave-it-healthcheck.

Use your findings, pull together your dream team and explain to your senior team why this is important not only for the mental wellbeing of their employees, but also for improving staff turnover, the number of sickness days taken and low productivity.

If you are ready to make some bold work happiness moves, head over to www.loveitleaveit.co to find out about my corporate training and toolkits.

I'm a team member or employee

You have read this book and feel energized to start making your working day feel good. However, you've noticed your manager is stressed out and has little time to make the differences you seek. Don't wait for them to start making changes – be the changemaker yourself.

Complete the starter happiness health check overleaf for yourself and five colleagues (of different levels and departments). This is the first step towards drawing up a proper LILI plan and strategy to make some changes you wish to see and get the help you think the team needs.

If you are ready to create better conversations, processes and systems at work to support your personal growth, career development and wellbeing at work, see www.loveitleaveit.co for more resources, tools and information. You can be the changemaker and start a LILI movement!

Starter happiness health check

Use this mini happiness health check to get a sense of where the happiness levels might be taking a nosedive or where everyone is genuinely very happy.

Send this to your chosen group of individuals and set aside roughly 30 minutes to complete it. Ask people to rate their scores from 1 to 10.

In addition, add a few notes under each question to explain their scores – keep the notes short and snappy – you want immediate gut reactions and insights. You can then use the learnings as a springboard for a later discussion in which you can decide on the required action points.

1. Head and heart
Answer on a scale from 1 (not at all) to 10 (a great deal)
To what extent do you have the ability to control key facets of your job?
Do you feel blocked from doing your best at work?

2. Communicate and connect
Answer on a scale from 1 (not at all) to 10 (extremely well)
To what extent are innovative ideas and knowledge spread across your company?
Do you feel you can connect with people at your company?

3. Work and life
Answer on a scale from 1 (not at all) to 10 (a great deal)
To what extent are you able to get creative in your job?
Do you feel inspired and proud to work at your company?

4. Digital and mindful
Answer on a scale from 1 (not at all) to 10 (a great deal)
To what extent are the surroundings and work conditions of the office energizing you and elevating your wellbeing?
Would you say you suffer from technological distractions?

5. Team

Answer on a scale from 1 (not at all) to 10 (a great deal)

To what extent do you enjoy working with the people in your team?

Do you receive help and support from your team when you need it?

6. Leader

Answer on a scale from 1 (not at all) to 10 (a great deal)

To what extent do you feel heard and seen by your manager?

Does your leader empower you to do your best work?

Do you receive constructive feedback on your work?

7. Company

Answer on a scale from 1 (not at all) to 10 (a great deal)

To what extent do you believe in the company values?

Is the job that you do contributing to society or a wider purpose?

Do you have clarity on the future direction of your company?

8. Work experience

Answer on a scale from 1 (extremely dissatisfied) to 10 (extremely satisfied)

How happy are you with your overall work life?

For a more detailed questionnaire and training resources for this, see www.loveitleaveit.co.

FURTHER READING AND SOURCES

Keeping momentum

If you have any questions, success stories or feedback, I'd love to know. Feel free to email me at sam@samanthaand.co

While I'd love to share tons of books, resources and websites, this book would be the size of a textbook. Thank God, therefore, for the internet. Head to www.loveitleaveit.co for resources, toolkits and subscribe to the newsletter.

If you want to spread the word you can do this in three ways:

- Writing a review massively helps another person in a similar situation to you make up their mind. Wherever you bought your book, whether on Amazon or elsewhere, please write a review or post it on Goodreads.
- Why not gift this book to your loved one, a friend, fellow co-worker or a family member .
- Share your 'Love It or Leave It' adventures and tag us on Instagram:
  @loveitleaveit_
  @samanthaand
  and on LinkedIn www.linkedin.com/in/clarkesl/

Recommended reading

Here are some reads to whet your appetite. See www.loveitleaveit.co for more.

Introduction
The 100-Year Life: Living and Working in an Age of Longevity by Lynda Gratton and Andrew Scott

Human + Machine: Reimagining Work in the Age of AI by Paul R. Daugherty and H. James Wilson

Humility Is the New Smart: Rethinking Human Excellence in the Smart Machine Age by Edward D. Hess and Katherine Ludwig

Work/life harmony
The How of Happiness: A Practical Guide to Getting the Life You Want by Sonja Lyubomirsky

Body of Work: Finding the Thread That Ties Your Story Together by Pamela Slim

Self Compassion: Stop Beating Yourself Up and Leave Insecurity Behind by Kristin Neff

The Resilience Factor: 7 Keys to Finding Your Inner Strength and Overcoming Life's Hurdles by Karen Reivich and Andrew Shatte

Working out where the pain is
The Dip: The Extraordinary Benefits of Knowing When to Quit (and When to Stick) by Seth Godin

Pause: How to Press Pause Before Life Does It For You by Danielle North

The Big Leap: Conquer Your Hidden Fear and Take Life to the Next Level by Gay Hendricks

Remind yourself that you are awesome
The 7 Habits of Highly Effective People: Powerful Lessons in Personal Change by Stephen R. Covey

So Good They Can't Ignore You: Why Skills Trump Passion in the Quest for Work You Love by Cal Newport

Do More Great Work: Stop the Busywork and Start the Work That Matters by Michael Bungay Stanier

The path to loving what you do
Deep Work: Rules for Focused Success in a Distracted World by Cal Newport

Radical Candor: How to Get What You Want by Saying What You Mean by Kim Scott

The Skills: From First Job to Dream Job – What Every Woman Needs to Know by Mishal Hussein

When you've lost that loving feeling
This is Marketing: You Can't Be Seen Until You Learn to See by Seth Godin

Side Hustle: Build a Side Business and Make Extra Money – Without Quitting Your Day Job by Chris Guillebeau

Range: How Generalists Triumph in a Specialized World by David Epstein

You've got this!
The Art of People: The 11 Simple People Skills That Will Get You Everything You Want by Dave Kerpen

Wisdom at Work: The Making of a Modern Elder – How to Reinvent the Second Half of Your Career by Chip Conley

Breaking the Habit of Being Yourself: How to Lose Your Mind and Create a New One by Dr Joe Dispenza

Sources

Introduction

Page ix

'The future will demand that you know…'

The Future of Jobs Report 2018 – World Economic Forum

www3.weforum.org/docs/WEF_Future_of_Jobs_2018.pdf (Accessed 4 November 2019)

Chapter 1

Page 6

'When was the last time you allowed yourself to just play?'

Brown, S. and Vaughan, C., *Play: How It Shapes the Brain, Opens the Imagination, and Invigorates the Soul*, J P Tarcher/Penguin Putnam, 2010

Chapter 2

Page 12

'Deloitte's Global Mobile Consumer Survey (Q4 2017) revealed that 34 per cent of us are checking our phones within 5 minutes of waking up and 48 per cent of us are responding to emails regularly between 2 and 3am.'

Deloitte's Global Mobile Consumer Survey (2017)

https://www.deloitte.co.uk/mobileuk2017/assets/img/download/global-mobile-consumer-survey-2017_uk-cut.pdf (Accessed 4 November 2019)

Chapter 4

Page 32

'Gallup reports that 30 per cent of employees have a best friend at work.'

'Your Friends and Your Social Wellbeing', *Business Journal*, August 2010

https://news.gallup.com/businessjournal/127043/friends-social-wellbeing.aspx (Accessed 4 November 2019)

Page 48

'Stress, depression or anxiety accounted for 44 per cent of all work-related cases of ill health.'

Health and Safety Statistics: Key figures for Great Britain (2018/19)

www.hse.gov.uk/statistics/ (Accessed 4 November 2019)

Page 49

'What happens when we get stressed at work?'

NHS UK

https://www.nhs.uk/conditions/stress-anxiety-depression/understanding-stress/ (Accessed 4 November 2019)

Chapter 6

Page 95

'Research by Paul MacLean, a physician and neuroscientist at Yale University, that first indicated we have three brains, each with "its own special intelligence, its own subjectivity, its own sense of time and space and its own memory".'

Andreas, K., *The Concept of the 'Triune Brain'*

https://www.interaction-design.org/literature/article/the-concept-of-the-triune-brain

Chapter 7

Pages 125–6

'The tech sector is constantly reinventing what career progression paths look like for creatives, developers, strategists and managers.'

https://monzo.com/blog/2019/01/07/progression (Accessed 4 November 2019)

Page 126
'Set up a meeting with your manager to address how you can take your work to the next level. DO NOT MENTION PAY YET. Address what you love about your work, your current status and abilities and that you are keen to take yourself to the next level.'
Berg, J. M., Dutton, J. E. and Wrzesniewski, A., *What is Job Crafting and Why Does It Matter?* https://positiveorgs.bus.umich.edu/wp-content/uploads/What-is-Job-Crafting-and-Why-Does-it-Matter1.pdf (Accessed 4 November 2019)

Chapter 8
Page 130
'What does it mean to have a positive, growth mindset? Carol S. Dweck, a psychologist at Stanford University, created the 'mindset theory' as a way to interpret the effects of the beliefs that individuals hold regarding their intelligence and their capacity to educate and learn new things.'
Dweck, Dr C., *Mindset: Changing the Way You Think to Fulfil Your Potential*, Robinson, 2017

Page 134
'Monitor your moods, your health and your needs for greater productivity, focus and alleviating stress.'
Fredrickson, B., *Positivity: Groundbreaking Research to Release Your Inner Optimism and Thrive,* Oneworld Publications, 2011 and Goleman, D., *Emotional Intelligence: Why it Can Matter More Than IQ*, Bloomsbury, 1996

Page 135
'Misery loves company and when we get stuck in complaining, others join in and it's a downward spiral.'
Jordan, A. H., Monin, B., Dweck, C. S., Lovett, B. J., John, O. P. and Gross, J. J., 'Misery Has More Company Than People Think: Underestimating the Prevalence of Others' Negative Emotions' *Personality and Social Psychology Bulletin*, December 22, 2010 https://www.ncbi.nlm.nih.gov/pmc/articles/PMC4138214/ (Accessed 4 November 2019)

'Could you join a programme offered by Remote Year or Unsettled?'
https://remoteyear.com
(Accessed 4 November 2019)
and https://beunsettled.co
(Accessed 4 November 2019)

Page 137
'Mihaly Csikszentmihalyi, a Hungarian-American psychologist, discovered that people find genuine satisfaction during a state of consciousness called flow.'
Csikszentmihalyi, M., *Flow: The Psychology of Happiness: The Classic Work on How to Achieve Happiness,* Rider, 2002

'Great apps like Focus at Will create and curate music specifically based on your behaviour traits and neuroscientific data on what promotes the best in focus, productivity, efficiency and happiness, so you've got no excuse not to finish that report and stay in the zone to smash through your to-do list.'
https://www.focusatwill.com
(Accessed 4 November 2019)

Page 138
'We can spend a lot of wasted time processing an argument so that the issue just goes round and round in our heads keeping us up at night. The better solution is to step away from whatever we are stuck on and do something else. This is what's known as Combinatory Play'
Juma A., *Why Einstein Used Combinatory Play & How You Can Too*
www.alyjuma.com/combinatory-play/
(Accessed 4 November 2019)

Page 139
'Choosing to take up hobbies beyond your realm of expertise keeps your brain nimble and you happier.'
Ratey, J., *A User's Guide to the Brain: Perception, Attention, and the Four Theaters of the Brain,* Vintage, 2002

'By learning a new hobby, you go through the four cycles of learning discovered by Noel Burch, an employee at Gordon Training International.'
https://trainingindustry.com/wiki/strategy-alignment-and-planning/the-four-stages-of-competence (Accessed 4 November 2019)

Chapter 11
Page 203
'I learned the concept of my monthly income from Ann Wilson, The Wealth Chef and international finance coach, whose mission it is to empower men and women to have more financial literacy.'
Wilson, A., *The Wealth Chef: Recipes to Make Your Money Work Hard, So You Don't Have To,* Hay House, 2015

Page 205
'For those of you who are thinking about starting a business or already running one and want to create an automated system for your personal and business finances you should read the brilliant book by Mike Michalowicz.'
Michalowicz, M., *Profit First,* Portfolio, 2017.

Page 220
'"What did you fail at this week?" I heard Sara Blakely of Spanx talk about how her dad would ask her this question at the dinner table each week so that they could learn the value of failure.'
'Spanx founder: My dad encouraged me to fail' https://www.youtube.com/watch?v=_TeV9op6Mp8 (Accessed 4 November 2019)

Page 222
'As Elizabeth Day, author and podcaster of How to Fail with Elizabeth Day, *states, in a climate where success is the all-consuming aspiration, it becomes increasingly difficult to try new things or take risks. But failure has taught me lessons I would never otherwise have understood.'*
Pantony, A., 'All Over the Gaffes: Why Failing Isn't So Bad Anymore' https://www.standard.co.uk/lifestyle/esmagazine/all-over-the-gaffes-why-failing-isnt-so-bad-anymore-a4217361.html (Accessed 4 November 2019)

Chapter 12
Page 228
'The famous stoic, Seneca, wrote: "Let us prepare our minds as if we'd come to the very end of life. Let us postpone nothing. Let us balance life's books each day… The one who puts the finishing touches on their life each day is never short of time."'
Seneca, *Penguin Great Ideas: On the Shortness of Life,* Penguin, 2004

Page 229
'As Shunryu Suzuki, founding father of Zen Buddhism in the US, states: "in the beginner's mind there are many possibilities, but in the expert's there are few"; that's all I'm asking you to think about.'
Suzuki, S., *Zen Mind, Beginner's Mind* Shambhala Publications Inc, 2011

INDEX

F

G

H

I

J

K

L

M

ACKNOWLEDGEMENTS

'It takes a village to raise a child!'

This book baby definitely had a massive support system to bring it to life.

Big thanks to my mega family who have prayed for and with me, visualized, consulted, coached, listened patiently, proofread, cooked and fed me when I was too tired or sick, provided inspiration with a dose of tough talk and loved me on my irritable days:

Akala
Amy Dick
Anita Borvanker
Anne-Marie Springer
Bianca Miller-Cole
Chanelle Newman
Chiron Cole
Dad and Mum
Della Michelle
Dominique Antiglio
Dorett Clarke
Emma Sexton
Fiona Buckland
Francis Lee
Freddie Harrel
Frederique Stephanie
Irene Moore
Jenny Garrett
Kate Nightingale
Kemi Akinbola
Kevin George
Ladi Delano
Lea Woodward
Leila Shokuhi
Letesia Gibson
Lotte Jeffs
Lucy Wern
Marianne Cantwell
Mark Leruste
Mei-Lin Rawlinson
Michy Kintu
Natalie Campbell
Peishan Chen
Petra Velzeboer
Ronke Oke
Tiwirayi Magwenzi
Tutu Amoye
Vanessa Belleau
Vanessa Brown
Vanessa Sanyauke
Winnie Awa
Yasmine Haimovici

Thanks to my editor, Claudia Connal, who allowed my vision to unfold, created order to my crazy, and patiently waited as deadlines came and went. To Sybella Stephens for all her work pulling the elements together to take us over the finish line. Juliette for bearing with me as we went back and forth on covers, but we did it! To Caroline and Caro for all your marketing magic. Equally I'd like to thank all the unknown faces I've never met who had a hand in bringing this book to life, and Hachette and Octopus for the opportunity to share my message. To my agents, Alice Saunders who saw something in me back in 2016, nurtured it and pushed me to keep believing in my voice, and Ben Clark who helped me see the gem in 'Love It or Leave It' and took us home to the win.

Immense gratitude to my clients, faces I've never met on my newsletter list, and all the beautiful humans I've spoken to on social media, at talks, workshops and events – you make my heart sing and give me wings!

To my awesome team who kept the ship afloat while my mind wandered away into book land: Riley McGhee, Em Romano, Jessica Nelligan, Gemma Sewell and Caz Wilson.

To everyone at Wildcard Cafe, for free mint teas and endless toasted banana bread that sustained me as I wrote for hours on end.

Finally, to my readers – thank you for buying this book. I hope this helps you find work happiness and please, please, please share the gems you learned here to help someone else too.

Love & hugs
Samantha xxx